My Life in His Hands

Sarah Louise Rosmond

This book was first published in the United Kingdom 2016.

My Life in His Hands © was republished in the United Kingdom in 2017.

This is Sarah's story in her own words.

Introduction...

This is what I remember.

I have been told that when terrible things happen to us we tend to block them out, I wish that was the case for myself. Unfortunately, I can remember my childhood as if it was yesterday, and it is funny that when I am telling you my story it is almost like it was a past life of mine. I know it all happened, but I soon learnt how to detach myself from the situation; which helped an awful lot while writing this story for you. I have never been able to talk about my past and you will learn while reading this book that even when I did speak out I was never heard. After having my own children and realising that, this is my life and I am now in control of my own life. This made me realize, that it is finally time for me to tell my story.

I found that once I started writing this book; I could just switch off to everything else going on around me. I found writing therapeutic. I now know it is good to get it out, and talk about my childhood and writing this book has helped me heal in so many ways. A handful of people know the outline of my upbringing, but the words in this book is the full story, or as least everything I remember in detail.

If my book can help just one person, then I feel that my horrible childhood might have had a purpose
 and not just a big horrid punishment. I will say that, I have no regrets, what happened in my life has happened and can never be undone.

I have tried to not go into too much detail when talking about the abuse scenes, to try and make my story easier to read. Abuse happens everywhere, and sometimes it is staring you straight in the face and you still might not see it, but I now know that life can throw anything at me and I will get through it. My past has made me the strong woman I am proud to be today.

'Everything happens for a reason and I truly believe that'

– Sarah Louise Rosmond xxx

Acknowledgements

I have many people in my life I wish to thank for getting me this far. First, I must thank my small amount of family who have stood by me throughout all of this. If I am honest it did take for me to write this story for even my own mother to know the full extent of my abuse and since knowing the truth she has been my major support and still is to this day.

I want to thank my partner for never using my past against me and for supporting me while I was writing this story. I am sure at times he was just as hard for him. He is the one man in this world who honestly made me realized that my past is where it belongs; in the past.

I would like to thank the author of 'A child called it' Dave Pelzer. His true story captivated me as a young adult and made me see that abuse is never okay, no matter how tame or serve it is, and also to the book man from my local market who had advised me to write my own story and so My Life in His Hands started.

My biggest thank you, should go to you, my reader. Without you my story would never be heard, and I am so grateful to each and every one who has taken the time to sit down with my book. For all the tears that will be shed I will apologies in advance. Just know that what happened to me made me the strong woman I am today, strong enough to share my story with you.

Sarah xxx

ISBN: 9781999900137

CONTENTS

The Sarah Rosmond Story (Part One)

Other titles include

My Life in his Hands

A Mile in my Own Shoes

Where will my journey end?

In the Beginning...

One of my first memories as a child, I must have been just over three and a half years old; we lived on a small council estate in Crosby, Isle of Man. It was May 1981, and it was a few weeks off my fourth birthday. I was super excited as my mum had told me she was going to buy me the new Barbie; I had seen the doll on the television, but mum said if I was good for a few more weeks. Not that she would have known if I was well behaved anyway because she was never at home herself.

Mum was out a lot at her boyfriend's house or something, but she was still young and was only seventeen when she had me. To be fair, my Nan was more than happy to look after me, and I think she enjoyed having a little person about the house. Since I could remember it was always my Nan who had raised; she would wake me in the morning with my bath ready and fresh ironed clothes waiting on the antique rocking chair in the corner of my bedroom. In the other corner of my room was a dark wooden chest with a lock on it and my bed was in the middle of the room with a pile of hand knitted blankets folded at the bottom of my big bed. I was never allowed in the chest but often wondered what my nanny kept in there.

My Nan woke me up just as always, but this morning she seemed stressed as she rushed around me.

'Get up now please' I looked at her with confused, sleepy eyes, and she repeated 'Please get up Sarah before your mum starts again,'

I was even more confused now, I thought my mum was out all weekend, it was a Saturday, and she was never normally at home on a Saturday.

I climbed out of bed, expecting to get ready for my bath but my nan just looked at me and said 'Sorry, no time for a bath today!'

I was only three and was used to my morning routine. I had a bath every morning, so I stood there. I could feel the tears well up inside me as I start having a mini tantrum. I was stamping the floor and demanding my morning bath, crying because I wasn't getting my way. Just then my mum walked in. She had black shiny high heeled shoes on with open toes and three-quarter length denim trousers and her favorite blue flowery blouse; mum's hair was styled in a short reddish, brown curly bob and her make-up was smudged by her eyes. She looked sad, and I had guessed she had been crying, she asked me what all the noise is about, Mum, then snapped at my nan and told her she had a headache. I continued to cry and shout, and mum marched over to me, grabbed me by the arm and swung her hand towards me. Her voice was high pitched.

'Shut up Sarah, I have a headache.' and with that, I felt a hot burning sensation on my bum where she had just smacked me.

'Mum, please sort her out I have been at work all fucking night' she shouted.

'If that's what you call it' Nan replied sarcastically.

I ran back to my bed holding myself where the stinging was, I was curled up in a ball underneath my blanket holding my knees to my chest. I felt like my stomach was trying to escape my body as I lay there crying hard.

I was sobbing louder and louder, hoping that my nan would come and comfort me, but she didn't, and when I finally stopped crying, I could hear my mum and nan arguing outside my bedroom door.

'You slapped me you cow,' mum shouted.

'She is a little girl who doesn't need her mother, calling her horrible names and smacking her' my nan continued; her voice getting lower.

I could only make out some of their conversation, so I got out of bed and walked towards my door, which had been closed over. As I got closer I could hear my mum, she was growling in my nan's face.

'She is my fucking daughter. Not yours'. My nan laughed, and replied 'Start acting like it then, Laura'

With that my mum stormed off downstairs stamping her feet on each stair as she went down them with speed, then I heard the front door slam closed. I guess she had, had enough and walked out. My mum and nan never usually argued, or at least I had never really heard them, and I felt terrible, that I had caused all this, all because of my tantrum.

Mum was meant to be taking me out, as she always did on a Monday, but she said she wasn't in the mood and that we would go the following week. Mum had promised the week before that she was taking me the next week, so I was upset.
Our trip to town was something I looked forward to doing. I knew mum got paid money on this day because she would always take me to the post office.

It was the same every week; we would stand in the queue outside and wait for what seemed; like forever when you are only three years old, but, it was probably just ten minutes or so.

Once I had waited patiently, and we finally got to the counter, mum would get out a booklet and sign her name at the bottom, she would then pass it over to the lady sat on the other side. The lady would stamp the little yellow book and pass it back to mum with money inside it. I always said thank you when we were walking over to the sweet counter holding my mother's hand. Last week Mum asked for her cigarettes as usual and a 30p mix-up for me, but she always said no Bubble-gum. The person behind the counter would just nod and pass me my ready-made bag of sweets.

I didn't know what bubble gum was, but I was very curious. It sounded magical, but I was also a bit worried that I would have an explosion of soapy bubbles dripping out of my mouth if I ever dared to try it. The only bubbles I knew about, were when my nan would put too much shampoo in my hair at bath time. I hated the bubbles because they always got into my eyes and it stung. That didn't stop me being curious though.

So, after we got my sweets, we walked to the bus stop and waited for the bus to arrive. While we were waiting for the bus, mum would often rearrange her hair as the wind would have messed it up during the small walk from the post office.

I noticed a letter in her pocket while she fumbled in her bag for a bobble to tie her hair up. When I asked her who the note was for, she told me not to be nosey. I thought nothing more of it as the bus arrived. I would soon find out that the letter was about the change my life entirely.

As we headed to town, mum started fussing with my hair and said I needed to look as pretty as possible. I didn't know why but I just smiled at her, and she smiled back. I was sat gazing out of the window, admiring how sunny it was and how fluffy the clouds looked, I must have been daydreaming because my mum said she called me three times before I looked at her, I only heard her the once. We arrived at town center my mum scooped me in her arms and quickly jogged towards the large glass doors, there were about twenty of these big glass doors all with big white signs above them with a big green letter on each. I had guessed this is, so the buses knew where to park. As we ran towards the door, I was looking up and noticed we went through the letter S.

'S, mummy, S is for Sarah' I said with a big grin on my face.

'That's right' my mum replied smiling back at me. Thinking back my mum seemed very smiley that day. Inside the big bus station, mum had put me down and I found myself looking around at amazement every time we visited. As soon as you walked through the doors, everything was so bright and colorful. All the shops seemed so tall and oversized to me, but the stairs were my favorite part of all, as they were big metal stairs that somehow, moved all by themselves. You would stand still at the bottom, and it would just transport you all the way up to the top, just like that. I didn't know how but guessed maybe there were little fairies or something helping us up to the top, bear in mind I am only three and a half years old. Mum said it was a mix of a lift and stairs.

'Like a stair lift,' I said with a smile on my face, 'Sort of.'

When we got to the top she asked me if I was ready to put on my big smile again.

I was confused at first but then seen a tall skinny man wearing all black taking a photo of a group of boys, they looked a bit older than me. The four boys were sitting on wooden crates, and one was inside a cardboard box. I giggled because I thought they looked hilarious. We walked over and waited our turn. I wasn't sure if I had to sit in a box too, I looked around and seen the tallest umbrella I had ever come across, 'Maybe it is for a giant' I asked my mum, she looked down at me a scrunched up her face a little.

'Don't be silly' she smiled. 'Your bloody nan reads you too many fairy tales, Sarah. One day you will realize life isn't like that at all.'

I didn't know why but I felt like I was being told off, so I just accepted that she didn't like what I had said to her. As the boys were finishing their photo shoot, mum was undoing my coat and rearranging my hair again. She was fussing and fixing my dress in place.

It was my favorite dress; it was a light pink and white striped dress with a big collar which was fashionable in them days, and it had a soft bow on the front which I had always fidgeted with, never able to keep my hands still. I must have been tiny for my age, at the age of almost four I was still wearing age two clothes. This dress was handed down by one of my aunt's as it didn't fit my younger cousin anymore.

The dress looked new, and I loved it and felt very proud of myself as I walked up to the man taking the photographs. I was a little nervous as the man told me where to stand. He got a big furry rug out of a box and placed it over one of the big wooden crates, he then grabbed a cushion and put it behind the wooden crate.

I was asked to kneel and place my arms on the soft rug in front of me. It was ticking my arms, and I think he must have seen I was a little uncomfortable, so told me to sit with my right arm lying flat on the rug and my other arm under my chin but I didn't understand what he meant. Mum then came to my rescue and walked over, and she placed my hands and arms like the man had asked and it reminded me of the new ice skating Barbie doll I had seen on the adverts. The way my mum had just moved my arms was how I imagined posing my toy, so, I smiled to myself, and the man shouted over to me

'Perfect.' My mum moved out of the way, and the man stood behind the camera.

'Right little one, I want you to smile like that again, do you think you can do that for me?' I nodded my head with a smile and nearly wobbled off the big cushion; I got my legs comfortable again.
The camera was flashing a lot, but somehow, I managed to keep my big smile on my face as I daydreamed about me playing with my new toy, though the flashing was making me blink a lot.

After my photos had been taken, we went to a shop called Granada Stores. In there were big televisions and stereos, we had a good TV at home, but these seemed three times the size of me. I asked mum if we were in the shop to buy one.

'Don't be stupid, how I can afford one of them.'

She said shaking her head and smiling at me. After looking at a few more shops and mum not buying anything at all, we started to walk back towards the bus station.

Now I was baffled, as well as the post office and sweets; on a Monday, we would always go to the cinema or ice skating for a few hours, but we were walking in the wrong direction. We headed towards the escalator and mum had said that the photo had cost her more than she had expected and that we would have to go next weekend instead, providing she has any money left.

So, for mum to say that she can't be bothered to go to town again, you can probably understand why I had started to cry. It was my birthday in ten days. I was told that if I was well behaved, I could have the new Barbie I so desperately wanted, and I honestly didn't want anything else. Even when my nan had asked me what I wanted, I told her the same. I did say she could buy me some clothes instead. Thinking back, I must have done their heads in by now as I had been going on about this silly doll for over six weeks.

That night my nan was getting me ready for bed, and I was excitedly telling her about my pretty photo I had done the week before. I asked her if she had seen it, but she just looked at me puzzled and said she would ask my mum when she got home.

Mum had gone out again and was due to take me to the doctors for a check-up the next day. Seems silly but I enjoyed going to the doctors.

'Will she take me, doctor, tomorrow' I asked.

'I'm not sure what your mother has planned love tonight, she doesn't tell me anything lately.'

Nan tucked me into bed and kissed my forehead, she then stroked my nose and said goodnight. It was our routine every night at bedtime.

The next morning mum was at home, and she was dressed and ready to take me to my appointment. I enjoyed going to the doctors because I liked the toys. The rocking horse was my favorite of them all; you could tell it was old though, the fur had been worn down to the white plastic on most of the head and back; what hair was still on it was grey instead of white and all matted together. We arrived at the surgery, and I started to go in a mood because a spotty ginger kid was playing on the rocking horse, and that was the only reason I ever wanted to go to the doctors. As we were waiting for my name to be called, I asked my mum if my nan had seen the photo we had taken.

She turned to me with a look of horror and said 'No I was meant to tell you not to tell nanny, it was meant to be a surprise. She looked at me and smiled 'why, what did you say?'.
'Nothing' I explained,

'You obviously said summit' she snapped.

'I only asked if she saw my pretty photo, that's all mummy' I pleaded, but it was clear I had annoyed my mother.

The next morning, I woke up to the sound of my Mum and Nan arguing again. I stayed in bed and heard my nan walking up the stairs with my mum stamping her feet behind her. Nan walked into my room and shouted to my mum.
'We will ask Sarah, then shall we?'

Mum didn't say anything as nan started ranting at me.

'Your mother said you didn't have any photos taken; she says you are lying.'

She continued 'Why would you have a reason to lie? She asked.

I sat up in bed and rubbed my eyes. 'I did have my photo taken' was all I said.

They both walked out of my room, and my nan repeated,

'What's the big deal if you're not hiding anything, Laura?'

I'm not sure why my mum said I was lying, but it would all make sense to me soon.

The next day it was sunny outside, and my mum sisters had all met at my nan's house which was normal anytime the weather was beautiful. All us kids were ushered out to play. We were playing a game of chase, all us cousins were on one side, and the other kids from the square were against us. We were all having fun and giggling when a little dark-haired little boy decided to join in. At first, he was playful and fair. But as the game when on he started to get a little too rough, and when it was his turn to be on, he started chasing after me. I needed to be tagged, but I had already witnessed him pushing half of my family to the ground. I didn't want to play anymore and shouted this as he set out to chase me. I may have been tiny, but I decided to stand my ground, as the boy got closer I started to cry, fearing he would hit me. The nasty child walked straight up to me and pushed me to the ground as hard as he could. He then said I had to play because it was the rules, and that if I didn't then he would punch me in the face, I told him he wasn't allowed and that I would grass on him.

'Why don't you go and get your daddy then? You little cry-baby'. He snipped as I got back to my feet, tears streaming down my face.

'I don't have one' I shouted back at him.

'Ha-ha that's funny' he was pointing his finger in my face while I stood there wiping the snot from my nose.

'What is so funny' I heard my cousin Katie snap back, she was stood beside us by now.

'Poor little girls a bastard, that is funny' he shouted at me, I turned and ran into my house crying, closely followed by Katie.

As I barged into the door, my mum was standing in the kitchen with her sister's Eliza and Margo.

'What wrong with you now?' Eliza asked. I turned to my mum sobbing with tears covering my face.

'Why did you make me a bastard? I asked confused, she looked at me with just as much confusion on her face as mine and asked me what I meant.

I could hear Eliza laughing at me as I started sobbing again. Mum lent down and was wiping the snot away from my lips with her sleeve when Margo began to laugh as well. I could tell my mum was trying her hardest not to join in with the laughter and this made me smile, I looked towards the doorway and Katie was covering her mouth too. So, I knew what I had said must have sounded funny. Then, my auntie, Margo asked me to repeat the question.

'Why did mummy make me a bastard?' I asked expecting her to give me an answer I can understand.

'Who called you that? 'Eliza asked

'The boy outside said I was a bastard, I told him I didn't have a dad, and he said that made me a bastard' I explained.

'Why is that your mother's fault?' She asks.

I shrugged my shoulders and stood there waiting for something to be said, but the adults just looked at each other with amusement on their faces.

Katie tapped me on the shoulder and asked me to play in the back garden with her, so off we went out the back to play. Katie hugged me as we got outside and told me that she is going to beat the dark-haired boy up next time she sees him on his own. Katie is only five, but I believe her and smile

Birthday Surprises...

It was July 1987, midsummer and in the middle of a heat wave. The day before my fourth birthday and my nan had told me that my mum had a surprise for me. I had guessed as it was my birthday that she was talking about my presents, but then she told me that, that was what her and my mum had been arguing about, but she said. Hopefully, it was a pleasant surprise though, and that was the end of the conversation. I assumed that maybe they argued over what to buy me, so I didn't ask any questions. That evening mum put me to bed, and she sat in the rocking chair because she said she needed to talk to me about something. I sat up in bed and, smiled at her, sure she was going to tell me that I had been well enough behaved and deserved my new Barbie.

'I need to talk about your daddy' she said with a soft, gentle voice.

'I don't have one, I'm a bastard remember.' was my reply while smirking at her. I knew I was cheeky, but I didn't care.

Mum stood up and moved towards me, I flinched as I thought I was going to get a clip around the, back of the head, but she just sat beside me on the end of the bed.

'Your dad lives in another country and has a family of his own, but he wants to meet you.'

I am a bit unsure what she is trying to say so I just smile at her.

'Goodnight mummy' and I lay down and close my eyes.

'Goodnight' she sighs as she gets up and walks out of my bedroom, pulling the door slightly too, but still opened enough so the landing light can shine into my room. I'm not scared of the dark, but I still like a bit of light in my room.

The next morning, I wake up, way too early. Nan is still fast asleep, and it was dark outside. I looked out of the window, and I could see the stars twinkling in the black sky. I then took myself to the toilet, washed my hands and climbed back into my bed. As I lay there, I started to think about what my mum had said. That my dad wanted to meet me finally. I didn't know I even had a dad, and if I did have one, I had never heard anybody talking about him. I started to wonder what he might look like, talk like, how he might dress. I had remembered my mum saying that he lived in a different country, so, maybe he spoke in a different language or something. I had been thinking hard for so long that I hadn't noticed my nan wake up, not until I heard my bath running.

I walked onto the landing rubbing my eyes like I did most mornings and nearly walked into the toilet door. The hallway was very skinny, and we had a separate toilet and bathroom, but you couldn't open both doors at the same time because the corridors were too narrow.

'Careful, Sarah' I heard my Nan say as I just missed the door handle with my head.

'Are you ready for your bath,' she said.

I ran into the bathroom with the biggest smile on my face and hugged my nan's legs.
'I am four today' I said excitedly.

As I sat in the bath and waited for my Nan to finish rinsing the bubbles out of my hair I started thinking about meeting my new daddy again. I was waiting until she stopped pouring water over me and looked up at her.

'Do you know who my new daddy is?' I ask inquisitively.

'Yes, but I'm unsure if I should have this conversation with you. You are best talking to your mum about that one.' She replied. So, I left it at that.

I was sat at the kitchen table eating my sugar puffs when my mum walked down the stairs.

'Where's my birthday girl' she said.

I couldn't reply because I had a full mouth of cereal, so I just made a strange rumbling sound.

'In here' I shouted through to the hall when I had finally finished chewing what was in my mouth.

My mum walked into the kitchen with a big present wrapped in pink flowery paper. I pushed my bowl to one side and raised my arms up. I unwrapped my present as quickly as I could. Almost wetting myself, with pure excitement. Finally, I got my Barbie; I was screeching. As I pulled the paper off I seen that it wasn't the Barbie I hoped I was getting at all, it was a baby doll with nappies and bottle. Maybe I had been too naughty for the Barbie, but I was still happy enough with my baby. She was soft and cute with a real hair curl on her forehead. I decided to call her Suzie.

Mum then asked me if I liked it and I smiled 'I love my Suzie.'

While mum was helping get my birthday present out of the box for me, my nan had gone into the cupboard under the stairs and pulled out the present she had brought me.

'It's not much this year' she said as she passed it to me. It was a soft present, wrapped in shiny silver paper with a big pink bow on the front.

I decided that I should probably go to the toilet before I opened it and got myself down from my chair. As I walked out of the kitchen, I heard my nan ask where my mum managed to find the money for such a big present for me. I didn't understand my mum's reply. When I got back down the stairs my nan was making her cup of tea, but she didn't ask mum if she wanted one, so I guessed they, had words again. I opened the present that my nan had gotten for me, and inside I found a fluffy, white teddy bear. It was holding a red number four. I was happy and cuddled the teddy as hard as I could.

Later that day my mum was putting my coat on, she explained that we were going to the train station to meet my dad and that he has gone out, and found me the Barbie I wanted. I had never met this man I was to call my daddy, but already I had decided in my little young head, that I liked him because he had at least listened to what I had wanted for my birthday.

I guessed that my mum must have told him about the doll. Seven weeks I had been on at her, nearly every single day without fail. I liked Suzie, but she wasn't my Barbie. On the way, my mum was trying to 'explain things' to me, but I didn't understand what she was saying.
I remember asking her what he looked like and she said last time she saw him herself, he was a spotty teenager.

'Like the ginger boy at the doctors' I ask, 'Yes Sarah, exactly like that but imagine him older.'

We were on the bus on our way up to the town center, and I was apparently annoying my mum, asking her lots of questions about what color trousers is he wearing? And what color are his eyes? Mum just kept answering

'You will see him soon enough, so, just wait and see.'

Once we arrived in town, I knew we had to go up the magical stairs again, and I was wondering who was getting their photos taken today. At the top of the escalator though, I couldn't see the skinny man or the giant's umbrella. Instead, there were two small grey-haired ladies; they were selling colorful flowers and plants. The taller lady looked at me a smiled.

'What a pretty little thing' she said talking about me.

I start wondering why mum made me out to be a liar to nanny and why she told her I never had my photo taken. With the skinny man nowhere in sight, it had me thinking, that maybe my mummy was right, and perhaps I didn't have a photo taken, after all, maybe it was all a dream. Then I thought a little harder and told myself that it did happen. Why did my mum say it was a surprise for nan if it was all a dream? It didn't make any sense at all.
The train station was at least a ten-minute walk from the bus station. We seemed to get there a lot quicker than that, and I was so deep in thought that I don't even remember walking through the town center or walking over the two bridges to get to the train station.
I remember the grey-haired ladies and next thing you know we are stood on the platform waiting for my dad's train.

Time went so fast getting from town to the train station, but once we got to the platform it seemed like we were waiting there for hours, the train was delayed but only by twenty minutes, but to me, that sounded a lot longer. I was nervous, and I remember telling mum that I felt sick, but she just told me to stop complaining, it's meant to be a happy time she said. I was bored, and my stomach was like a washing machine spinning. I wasn't feeling happy at all; nervous and excited at the same time maybe, but confused is the word I would use to describe best how I was feeling.

The train finally pulled into the station. It was deafening and noisy. A few people that had been waiting on the platform, all started grabbing their bags and standing by the platform edge. Mum and I held back near the entrance to the station and waited. Everyone got off the train, and the people who were waiting with us on the platform had all boarded the train, but there was no sign of this man I was to call my daddy. The train engine started up again. I hid behind my mum's legs and clung on for dear life. I had convinced myself that the last time we were waiting on the train, that the wind was a big scary cloud. I had worried that the wind from the train departing, would be so high that it would drag my little body away with it. Making the big scary cloud eat me all up. I know now how silly that sounded, but at the tender age of four, your imagination could quickly take over, and the fear of the unknown can engulf anyone's feelings. I had an excellent imagination my nan had often said.

As the train pulled off down the track, mum was muttering stuff under her breath, but I couldn't understand what she was saying. She reached into her bag a pulled out her pack of twenty super kings; she lit her cigarette and muttered.

'Well it's typical that your dad hasn't turned up.'

I just looked up at her confused but didn't say anything.

'We can wait for the next train; it's due in twenty-five minutes, can you cope that long?' she asks.

I nodded my head and smile. I was getting more and more excited at the thought of playing with my new Barbie, if I was honest I didn't understand how vital meeting my new daddy was, I just wanted the Barbie. To be fair from my point of view, while living at my nan's, I was introduced to other men who I was told at the time, might be my dad, so why was this man any different. That makes my mum sound wrong, but I don't mean it that way.

My uncle would tell me his mates were my daddy, more so, to annoy my mum, and then my mum's boyfriend Mick was kind to me, and I had asked my mum if he was going to be my daddy. That was only a few months ago, and Mick said he would love to be my father. So, meeting this new man didn't seem like anything significant to me. He was yet another man that my mother knew. The train had finally arrived, while we were still stood by the entrance, I could see that we were the only people waiting and wondered if mum had come to the right station. Just as I was about to ask her, I noticed a train coming down the track. The train came to a stop, and the doors opened, quite a few passengers got off the train. I looked around at all the men wondering which one was my dad.
'Is my daddy here?' I asked my mum, and when she didn't answer I looked up, but she wasn't beside me anymore, I started to panic.

I could feel the bubbles in my belly, and my bottom lip started to shake. Then through my teary eyes, I noticed my mum talking with a man, so I walked towards her.

When I got beside her I seen a little boy, I guessed he must have been a bit older than me as he was taller, he looked at me with bright blue eyes, and I turned my head in shyness. I was looking back up at him from the feet up; he was wearing denim jeans and a big blue parker style coat with grey fur around the hood. I remember that because it was a very sunny day and I thought it was odd that he had this big jacket on when it was so warm. He was stood next to a lady; she was slim with curly brown hair and a mole on her face, she was quite small framed, similar build to my mum and stood about five foot tall. She was holding a baby, but I think he was asleep in her arms because I don't remember him making any sound. My mum noticed me and put out her hand for me to hold.

'There you are, Jason this is your daughter' He looked at me and smiled.

'Oh, you are a cutie' he said crouching down to my eye level.

He sounded weird, his voice seemed high pitched for a man, I remember thinking at the time. I looked at the down at my shoes nervously for a few minutes, but I could feel them all staring at me, so I closed my eyes. I opened them a few seconds later but kept my head down and said nothing. I could see out of the corner of my eye that the man had stood back up. The adults were talking to themselves, and I looked at the little boy and smiled. He made a grunting sound and folded his arms.

'Ignore him he is grumpy today' the lady with the baby said.

Her voice seemed a bit weird to me too; higher pitched like the man's voice. Mum then grabbed my hand, and we all started walking towards the bridge.

Back at the town center, mum had asked if I was hungry. I told her I wasn't, but the man said he was, and mum agreed that we would have some lunch while we were out. We walked from one side of the big town center to the other and stopped outside a minute while mum adjusted her hair again, we had to walk across a car park to get to the small shopping mall where the café was. Mum had told me before that she used to work in the restaurant long before I was born, and the owner gave her a discount. Once inside we walked towards the table by the only window in the café.

'This is the smokers table' she said to the couple.

We sat down at the large table and the lady holding the baby pulled out a chair and gently placed the baby who was still fast asleep in the chair wrapped up in a blue knitted blanket with only his face showing.
'Is that a doll?' I asked the lady.
She smiled at me. 'No this is Shane; he is your brother.' She said in a very matter of the fact tone.

My mum butted it. 'She's too young to explain all that to her.'

The lady didn't say anything back she just shook her head. After we had eaten, and the lady got her breast out to feed the baby that was now awake. I couldn't help but watch, even though mum had nudged me and said it was rude to stare, I couldn't help myself. I didn't know that you could feed a baby from your boob, I was only four, and this would get explained to me later that evening.

Once the baby was fed, we all stood up to gather our belongings and started to make out way back towards the town center.

We were stood outside a clothes shop and the man who I
was told I should call my daddy, took his rucksack off his
back and rummaged inside it. I was young and being an
inquisitive child, I walked over to him, to see what he was
doing. I could see a wrapped up present and guess it was
for me and started excitingly jumping up and down on the
stop.

'Calm down Sarah,' my mum said to me patting me on the
head as a jumped up.

My dad passed me the present, and I sat on the floor to
open it, the boy who was moody earlier had sat beside me
watching me open my gift, I was so excited that was until I
pulled all the paper off that was.
He hadn't brought me the Barbie doll mum said he was
getting; he had got me a Barbie, but it was the ballerina
one instead. I should have been happy, but instead, I
threw the doll on the floor and shouted.

'I didn't want that one.'

With that outburst, the man had clipped me round the
back of my head and called me an 'ungrateful bitch.'

I started to cry, and my mum told me it was my fault for
'being so rude.'

How could she say I was rude? I had waited for what
seemed like a lifetime for the Barbie advertised on the TV
and mum, and nan both said I had been a perfect little girl
and that I would get it.

That morning when I didn't get it off either of them, I was
told that my 'dad' had bought it for me. Dad – funny
really, I didn't know this man, and from what I had just
witnessed and felt, I was unsure if I liked him or not.

He was around when I was a new-born, but then he joined the army and left my mum for another lady. I guessed at the time that the small lady with the mole.

'The lady that stole your daddy' she would often snap when talking about him in the past.

I thought it was against the law to steal, and often wondered why my mummy didn't ring the police on the lady. The adults were talking among themselves again, but by this point, the baby was crying, and the lady was bouncing her body up and down trying to settle him in her arms.

'We are going to have to go soon, Jason' I heard her say.

With that, we had all started to walk again. We got to the bus station and said our goodbyes. Mum and I got on the bus and waved to them, as the engine on the bus fired up. My dad blew a kiss, and my mum put her hand up in the air as if she was catching something and then placed her hand on her lips. I wasn't sure who he blew the kiss for, but my mum had told me it was for her, mum was smiling like a child all the way home. She was acting like a big kid, but she was only twenty-one at the time. Mum had given birth to me, at the early age of seventeen and had dropped out of school while carrying me. She gave birth just three weeks after her eighteenth. My dad was a few years older, and they had only been dating for a while when she had conceived me.

The journey home on the bus was a bit awkward. Mum didn't talk, and my head was so full of questions, but I didn't know what to say, so we sat in silence.

My New Routine...

The most prominent change I had noticed in the months after meeting my dad was that mum seemed to be at home a lot more often, no more going out on a Thursday evening and returning in the early hours of the Monday night. She seemed bubblier and always smiling. She was getting on with my nan, a lot better too, less shouting anyway, they still bitched at each other, stupid little insults, usually about something I had said or done.

They were disagreements about my upbringing mainly. Nan had a different approach to raising me, it was all about strict routine with her, whereas mum thought that's was boring for a little girl and liked being spontaneous. It was raining outside, and nan had gone out to the local shops to do some shopping. I was meant to go with her, but for some reason, I ended up staying behind with my mum. My auntie Eliza was round with her little boy, Brandon. He was only a few years or so younger than me. I remember sitting in the living room, we were engrossed in the television, Roland Rat was on, and at the time it was one of the funniest things I had ever seen on TV.

My mum was upstairs packing my clothes in a suitcase. I didn't ask why I just remember thinking that we were all going on holiday. It wasn't that far from the truth. I was to find out later that day, my mum and I were moving out of my nan's house, I wasn't told where though so guessed we had our own home. Mum had been saying for at least a year, that she would be happier in her place, just her and me.

The next morning, everything seemed as it should. Nan had got me up, gave me my bath and got me ready for the day; mum had finally got out of her bed at about ten past ten. I was sat in the kitchen, and being ever so quiet while concentration hard on my drawing, I had my jumbo crayons and paper. Nan liked to encourage me to draw pictures and had got me a cushion from the sofa so that I could reach the kitchen table. Nan then started making my lunch; she had said that she was preparing it early for me because she had errands to run at one o'clock. I could hear my mother upstairs giggling like a school girl. She had someone upstairs with her; they must have got back late at night while I was asleep. I climbed down from my chair and went to walk out of the kitchen when my nan piped up

'And where do you think you are going, young lady?' she said sternly.

'Just to the toilet' I replied.

I didn't need the toilet I was just curious and wanted to see who was upstairs. As I walked passed my mums bedroom, I could hear them whispering to each other. I peeped my head around the small gap in the door, and I could see my mum and dad with tiny clothes on. They looked like they were playing a game of cowboy and Indians. I guessed mum was the horse because she was on all fours and making weird growly noises and my dad was knelt behind her, smacking her bum and repeating.

'That's my girl.'

Just then I heard my nan shouting up the stairs.

'Foods ready. Sarah, you make sure you wash your hands before you come down these stairs. Do you hear me?'

'Yes, nanny.' I shouted back down to her.

I was still standing outside my mother's bedroom door when I had shouted, but then I heard one of my parents coming towards the door. I froze for a second, but I suddenly heard the creaky floorboard by my mum's wardrobe and darted straight into the bathroom. Before heading downstairs, I had another peep through my mum's door. I saw my dad stood in the doorway with a towel around him as he had just had a bath. I felt a rush of fear that I might be caught and rather than head down the stairs, I ran back into the bathroom and closed the door behind me; I could hear someone in the toilet in the room next door. Dad must have needed a pee, so I waited until I heard him finish.

Now I needed the bathroom myself, the chain flushed, but I still waited till I could hear footsteps. I was half expecting them to go back into my mum's bedroom, but instead, I mentally followed each beat down the stairs. Once I knew the coast was clear, I opened the bathroom door. I remember thinking to myself while washing my hands that whoever did use the toilet didn't wash their own hands, because I was in the only room with a sink in it, apart from the kitchen.

Meanwhile downstairs, Nan had dished up our food, my mum and dad had sat down at the kitchen table. It was too early for lunch, but my mum was late for her breakfast, so nan called this meal my brunch.

I wasn't all that hungry as I had eaten coco pops just a few hours before. I walked up to the table and pulled out the chair beside mum, she didn't notice me struggling with the weight of my chair, and nan had her hands in the sinking, washing the dishes.

When I finally got up to the table, I noticed my mum and dad kept looking at each other a little shifty, then looking over towards my nan, who had her back to us. I think they were whispering so my nan couldn't hear.

The smell of our home cooked breakfast filled the house, the smell of a full English breakfast still makes me think of my nan to this day. When she had finished serving, she placed my dinner in the fridge to cool it down. We were all sat down at the table. I saw my dad put his hand underneath the table, he was rubbing my mum's leg, and she was giggling for him to stop. My nan was annoyed with them both and forcefully stood up, pushing her plate away from her with her hands, and knocking her chair on the floor.

'It's bad enough you are back in her life, without rubbing my nose in it' she shouted at my dad, before he could answer her back she started shouting again. 'And what about your kiddie and missus in Ireland, you forgot about them have you!'

My dad stood up 'You know fuck all' he paused 'I love Laura, and we are together whether you like it or not' He sounded very stern.

'Sarah, go to your room' my mum said, apparently not wanting me to hear the argument, so I climbed down from the table keeping my eyes firmly on the floor.

'No, you stay here' I heard my nan say.
I didn't know who to listen to, so I just stood in the doorway, still staring at the brown mark on the floor. I could hear noises, but I must have zoned out slightly as I stood there. The adults all continued to argue.

It when on for a least ten minutes, the whole time I just stood in the doorway not listening, but I still knew why they were shouting. The gist of it was, my dad had left his wife and the two boys in Ireland and decided he wanted to be with my mum. They argued a lot in that few minutes about me and how my nan wanted them to leave but she wanted them to let me stay with her. That wasn't going to happen anytime soon, now was it?

That evening it was just my nan and me at home, she had put me to bed and was reading me my bedtime story like she always did. Thinking back now she was trying to say her goodbyes to me, but I was only four, and all I wanted to do was lay down with my Suzie doll and go to sleep. My nan looked sad as she headed downstairs to watch her programs. Some evenings when I had been well behaved all day, I would have the special treat of watching 'Emmerdale Farm' with nan. It was her favorite program I think because it was the only one I ever heard her talk about, and she even let me snuggle up in her chair with her.

While I was upstairs, I could hear her crying, so I got out of bed to investigate. I crept down the stairs as quietly as I could, and when I got to the bottom of the stairs, I peeped my head around the living room door.
Nan was rolled up on the sofa, she looked asleep, but I could hear and see her sobbing uncontrollably. I walked towards her, and she stopped crying, sat upright and wiped her tears on her napkin which she always kept up her sleeve.
I asked her why was she so sad and she said whimpering 'They are taking you away tomorrow, and that makes me sad. So, so sad. I love you, Sarah.' She said emphasizing the 'you,' I was confused, and I didn't want to leave my nan either.

Everything at that point was so messed up, no wonder I was confused. I had gone through a routine and knowing what I was doing each day to all this, messed up, and confused household, bath times were rushed, and bedtime came earlier than usual. I remember wondering what my nan was talking about, and wondered why she kept telling me that she loved me. I knew my nanny loved me because she would tell me every night before bedtime. So, I was a little confused why she kept repeating it that night.

The next morning, my nan had stayed in bed, and instead, mum had got me up and dressed. While she was brushing my hair, I told her about me seeing nanny crying the night before, and mum answer to it all was

'Oh well, she will get over it, you came out of my fanny, not hers.'

She used that saying a lot, but I never really knew what she meant. I could see that mum was upset, but she had this problem with ever showing it. I know that comment was out of anger as they had fallen out the night before, so I just smiled at my mum in the reflection of the mirror. We finished getting ready and dad was waiting outside with our bags. Mum had convinced me that moving was a big adventure and she told me how we would need to travel on a bus, a train and a boat all on the same day. By that point, she had won me over ultimately, and I was excited. We were getting our coats and hats on ready to leave. It was mid-October so quite nippy outside. Mum walked to the bottom of the stairs and shouted up.

'Well, you not coming to wish us well.'
She heard no reply.

'Well suit yourself, mother. We're off now.'

With that she held my hand and opened the front door, we stepped out on to the porch, and she shouted into the hallway.

'Fine then.'

I didn't want my nan to think I was moody with her too and I wanted to say goodbye and give my nan a big kiss, but mum had hold of my hand.

'I love you too, nanny' I shouted as we walked out of the door.

'Bye mum, lovely knowing you' my mum said as she closed with her other hand.

She then turned to me, smiled, 'Let our adventure begin.'

We had traveled on the bus and walked through the town center to get to the train station.

'This is where I first met you' I said to my dad.
'Not the first time, you met me, but possibly the first time you can remember.' He replied with a smile.

'Are you looking forward to living with daddy?' my mum asked.

I shrugged my shoulders and looked at the floor. Just then our train had arrived, we boarded the train and were lucky enough to find the empty seats with a table in front of them, there were only six of these style seats on the whole train.

'That was lucky' mum said, winking at my dad.

I climbed over the seats and sat by the window.

My dad asked if I wanted my coloring things out of the bag, I said no. He took them out of the bag anyway and placed the pad and jumbo crayons on the table in front of me. I crossed my arms in a huff and looked out of the window.

We had to get off the train after a short ten-minute journey, and then took a bus to the port where we would be getting on the boat to Ireland.

I don't remember the boat trip if I'm honest, my mum said I had slept most of the time. I just remember waking up in the soft playroom. The room was full of big bean bags, the walls were all padded in bright blues and greens, and the carpet was navy blue with yellow circles about the size of dinner plates all over it. I was in the room on my own, and I remember panicking. Just as I started to cry my dad had walked in and told me it was time to go. As I stood up to go to the door my leg felt all funny, it was all prickly and hurt to touch, and as I tried to stand on it, I wobbled and fell to the floor in floods of tears.

My dad sighed and picked me up off the floor. He told me to stop being so silly, it was only pins and needles, and I would be okay. I asked why did he put needles in me and he laughed.

'No silly, it's just a saying.'

He was still giggling to himself when he had seen my mum and told her what had happened. She looked at me and shook her head in disbelief.

After we got off the boat, we needed to get a taxi, and mum said we were going to stay with my dad's sister, my Auntie Amy. I had heard that she had four children all close to my age.

Veronica was about seven; Sally was five, Paul Jr was four the same age as Naomi, and I was two.

Amy had a husband called Paul, but he was always out working so I didn't see him much and he never really got mentioned. When we arrived in Belfast, I had noticed that some of the houses had a big painting on the side of them and the curbstones were all varied colors. Green, white and orange. I had asked my dad why the floor was colored, and he just said the word 'territory' to me.

'You will understand one day' my mum said.
I turned my head to look out of the window, and I could see a big iron door, must have been the size of a small house, and outside were two men in combat clothes holding big guns. I was a bit scared, and I could see them staring at our taxi as we drove past. I hid my face for a few moments, and when I looked out of the window again I saw a flag I had recognized, it was blighted blue, with red and white strips, hanging in a house window and I noticed the curbstones were red, white and blue.
I wondered if the next road would be pink and yellow, but I was wrong. The following road we went past, looked scary, the houses were broken and looked all black and dirty. Walls from the b had been knocked down. Trees were lying in the middle of the roads and bins knocked over, rubbish everywhere. My dad asked the taxi driver what had happened. I heard the driver saying that a dealer got burnt out, they petrol bombed his house but took nearly the whole street out with it.

He continued 'IRA we think, killed four civvies.'

I didn't take much notice because I didn't know what civvies were and I was feeling very apprehensive about speaking.

As we pulled up outside my aunt's house, I could see her kids were playing in the garden.

The children were crawling in and out of a small concrete bunker, and they were filthy, like really, really dirty and completely covered in soot from the coal. You could just about make out they all had light blonde hair underneath all the grey dust. My nan would have never let me get so dirty, especially if we were expecting guests. Veronica or Vee for short was the first one to see us pull up outside and she ran into the house to tell her mum.

'Uncle Jason's home' she shouted.

Sally ran over to the car just as mum undone my seatbelt. I climbed down trying not to get my bright white dress anywhere near the soot-covered girl stood in front of me. As I moved out of the way and stood by the front of the car, Vee decided to give me a big hug; I didn't see her coming so wasn't able to release myself from her grip. 'Hello cuz' she said squeezing me tightly, her grasp pinching at my skin

'Get off me you're dirty' I said trying to wriggle from her.

When she finally let go of me, my dress was ruined. I had big dirty, grey marks all over the front of it and I started to cry. Mum and dad didn't notice me crying; they were too busy talking to the taxi driver about the blown-up houses we had seen around the corner, they were far too busy to care about me or my dress. Amy came out of the kitchen and led me into the downstairs toilet to clean up the mess her daughter had caused; she then shouted at her kids to go upstairs and wait for their bath. After I was cleaned, I was sent to the living room where my mum was sat down on the sofa. My dad was in the kitchen making a cup of tea for the adults. It was the first time I had met this side of my family, and I was missing my nan so when my mum asked if I was okay, I snapped that I hated it here.

I must have sounded ungrateful, and I was led out into the hallway by my dad's sister. Amy asked me what all the big fuss was about and I cried and told her how I was feeling. She then said to me that I also have a grandparent who lives a few doors away and that I would meet my granny the next morning. That was enough to get me out of my mood, and I was asked to wish my parents goodnight and head up to Vee's bedroom when a bed was made up on the floor for me. I kissed my mum goodnight and hugged her tightly. I then went to walk out of the room when Amy told me to give my dad a kiss and a hug too. I remember not wanting to, as I blamed this whole move on the man, but I did as I was told anyway.

We settled into family life very easy in Ireland. My entire dad's family lived within a ten-minute walk from each other, and my cousins became my best of friends. We did everything together.

I had started school for three hours a day and mum had a cleaning job at the factory where dad also worked. Her shift worked perfectly with my school hours. Life seemed perfect, and I didn't think about my nan as much as I had expected, the first week we had left in the Isle of Man, she was on my mind daily, but after a few weeks, I had gotten used to her not being around. I loved spending so much time with my mum who was usually at home with me.

Everything seemed to be going well, but that was all set to change as my mum and dad had managed to get their own house just a few doors away from my other Uncle who was called Derek. He had two older boys and a small dark-haired daughter, called Jody. She was a year or two younger than me, and they had a massive dog called Maxwell. I feared the dog so anytime I ever spent at their house was mainly spent in Jody's bedroom. Derek's wife was named Mary. I didn't like her, she always gave me horrible looks, and I had overheard her telling my mum that I was rude and unwelcome news for their precious little girl. I wouldn't have minded, but I hadn't been naughty at her house once, Derek was strict, and I was scared to play up.

In fact, Jody was going through a naughty stage, only being two and a half years old, she would kick off anytime anyone said no to her, so I'm not sure what they had against me. I know that when you are that age, it is hurtful to think that an adult doesn't like you. I know I cried that evening when my mum told me about what was said, and not because I felt like I was being told off, it was more so the fact, that Jody's mummy didn't like me even though I was always on my best behavior.

The Nightmare Began...

We had been living in Ireland for just over a year now. I was five and a half, and mum had only given birth to my baby brothers. She named her twins Daniel and Callum. Dad had lost his job a few months before and had started acting strangely; he seemed to respond even stranger at night time, with big wide eyes and talking faster than usual. He would stay up all night drinking beer and gossiping with his mate's downstairs.

While mum, on the other hand, was always sleeping, I think having twins took it out of her, and dad didn't seem to help them at all. During the day once when I wasn't at school I had seen dad putting a white powder in my mum's coffee, I wasn't sure why he would put talc powder in her drink and guessed it would taste all soapy. Mum always said it was used to make me smell nice after my bath, so I was confused. Just then my dad had seen me standing in the hallway.

'This will give her a boost' he said smiling to himself, as he walked past me.

Carrying the coffee upstairs and spilling half of it over himself, I had overheard him telling my mum, that he had something to wake her up. The twins were asleep in their crib in the living room so, I sat on the floor and watched the end of the video that had been playing.

'It's finished' I shouted at the top of my voice.

With that, the twins woke up crying.

I heard dad running down the stairs. I thought he was running to calm the babies down, but instead, he ran straight towards me and started slapping me around the head repeatedly, stopping for a second as I looked up at him. He had a look of outrage, as he looked at me and started smacking me even harder. I put my arms up to try and protect my face, but he pulled me up by my arms and slapped my bum that hard, that I was lifted, off my feet. I was screaming out in pain, but he was just shouting over me

'Shut up you, stupid bitch, shut the fuck up.'

He swung at me yet again. 'Stupid little bitch, I'm going to kill you if you don't shut the fuck up now.'

With that, he let go of me, turned around and walked calmly back upstairs where my mum was still hiding. I was sobbing like a baby, and the twins were again crying uncontrollably. Not that it made much difference. We were just ignored, as usual. I have since found out that my dad had been drugging my mum with amphetamines for three days.

As time went on I started to realize that a white powder my dad would have, the more aggressive he was towards me. I wasn't poorly behaved, but if I answered him back, or I didn't do what he said at that exact moment, I would suffer the consequences. I was getting older, so the smacking was getting harder, usually hitting me on my body so no one could see the marks. I'm not sure if that was deliberate or if it was just because I would always be coward myself into a small ball. It was less painful that way.

I had started to resent my mother too; to me, she just stood there and watched as this man beat her daughter right in front of her face time and time again.

How can a mum do that to her daughter?

Until one day I realized he was just as nasty to my mum as he was to me. I was seven years old by now and spent most of the time with my mum, even while she was at work. Mum was a barmaid at a local pub, and for some reason, my dad had refused to look after me in the evenings but said he didn't mind having the twins. I sat in the corner of the pub for the whole four-hour shift, and read my book; I was reading James and the giant peach because we were doing it at school at the time. I was so engrossed in the book and time had flown in. Mum finished her shift at 10:15 pm, but it was almost half ten by the time we outside. Dad was expecting mum, no later than 11 pm. We could either walk home which took a half hour or catch the bus which would guarantee we were back in time. We decided to wait for the bus. It was due at 10:39 pm, and we had got to the bus stop with plenty of time to spare. It was just our luck when the bus didn't turn up. By this point it was 10:47 and my mum kept looking at her watch; I could see on her face that she was worried sick.

'Are you ready for a jog?' she asked.

'Come on then mum; we can have a race' with that we set out for our sprint.

Almost straight away I got a stitch on my side and had to stop.

'Were going to be late' she shouted.

I pushed out my chest and ran as fast as I could to catch up with her. We were both, entirely out of breath by the time we had got back to the street, right beside our house, we got outside, and mum looked at her watch 11:02 pm.

Wow, we had run all the way home within fifteen minutes, that wasn't bad considering it would take a fully grown adult half an hour at least to walk back and I was only seven years old.

Mum was twenty-five, but she was petite build and still got asked how old she was when she ever went out to the pub. It was an awkward evening at the bar she works in, that got her the job in the first place. The owner had refused to serve my mum and had told her that her birth certificate wasn't hers. Back in the eighties, most people would carry their passports as identification, but mum didn't own one. She was turned down for alcohol and decided to apply for a passport. When she returned to the pub and told them that she was out of pocket just to prove her age, mainly out of her stubbornness more than anything, she was pleasantly surprised when the owner apologized and offered to pay her back if she fancied a few evening shifts.

Mum looked scared as we walked in through the front door, all the lights in the house were off in the house at it was silent.

'Your dad must be in bed' she whispered as she turned on the hallway light.

Dad wasn't in bed, he was standing by the living room door with his arms crossed, but all the lights off. He looked pissed off. He had this cold evil stare that sent shivers down my spine every time I saw it. It was the same look I had seen before time and time again when he was angry with me, and it was clear he was upset with my mum.

The man might have only been small himself, but none of us in the Rosmond family were ever that tall.

The adults were all between 5 and 6 foot at a push. Dad stood about 5 foot 6, small for a fully-grown man. He probably weighed no more than ten stone, but he was strong and a hell of a lot stronger when he was angry.

Dad walked towards us and me automatically coward myself into the corner by the front door. I squeezed my eyes closed and covered my head waiting for the beating to begin, but as I hid in the corner, I could hear my mum yelp out in pain. I opened my eyes and watched him drag her by the hair, to the bottom of the stairs and demanded she gets on her knees. She was begging him to stop, apologizing for being late and promised not to be late again but he just kept repeating.

'You're too late, you're too late.' He then walked towards me staring me straight in the eyes.

'You want to watch, you, stupid bitch' he sneered at me.

For the first time, I had heard my mum screaming at him to leave me out of the argument, that it wasn't my fault, but he didn't listen to her. He grabbed me by the hair and dragged me to the stairs where my mum kneeled on the floor.

'If you don't want me to beat the shit out of you as well I suggest that you sit down and shut the fuck up.'
He grabbed my face and put his nose on mine; his face was so close he looked like he had one eye; I was trembling with fear and whispered 'Yes' in acknowledgment. Dad pushes my face away so hard I had fallen back on the stairs and hurt my back, I started to cry. 'Do you like that?' he asked me.

'No' I shouted back, with that he kicked my mum in the ribs and told her.

'You better shut her fucking up Laura or she's next.'

'Please leave her alone' she begged. Instead he just kept kicking her and smiling at me.

From that moment on I knew we were trapped. My nightmare had only just begun. If my mother was powerless to him, then what hope did I have but to just sit there and watch her beg my dad to finish the beating so that she could go to bed. Thinking back now, she must have been getting beatings from him for years, by the way, she coped with it. Could it get any worse than this? I remember thinking as I lay in bed sobbing that night. I couldn't sleep as I relived the whole argument over and over in my head.

A few months later the whole family was getting ready for a big New Year's Eve party; it was a special time because for the first time all the family was together to celebrate. Amy and Derek put their heads together and rented a massive barn. Uncle Derek had an agenda as he had invited a few business friends along too, so, he wanted to look good, and that meant he had to splash the cash a bit. The room was a big massive open barn with fairy lights draped all over the exposed wooden beams.
It looked magical inside and out; the decorations had been left up from the previous Christmas party, the tree in the corner stood almost ten-foot-tall and had bows attached that were easily the size of my head.

There were loads of family members there, I knew most of them but there were a lot of strangers too, and I felt a little nervous. I could see my mum talking to my uncle Ronald, he was the eldest of my dad brother's, and he looked the wisest too with his big glasses and his ginger Santa style beard. So, I made my way to their table.

Mum was drunk and had been drinking Jellybean all night, Uncle Ron had offered me a swig out of the bottle, and I felt all grown up as I raised the bottle to my little lips. It was disgusting. Aniseed flavor and it burnt my mouth as soon as the liquid touched my tongue. No wonder my mum was drunk. Within minutes of the music starting my mum was on the dance floor. It was so embarrassing to watch. Everyone on the dance floor was doing line dancing and at the front was a lady, dressed in all the cowgirl gear, blonde curly hair hanging from her cowboy hat, teaching the guest all the dance moves. My mother thought she was better than the paid instructor and she honestly thought she was the best of the best and went straight up to the poor woman, and pushed her out of the way. She was wasted, and couldn't even stand up straight let alone dance. As the night went on everyone seemed to be having an excellent time, mum, on the other hand, was falling over tables and having an outburst of tears every now and again.

There were a few other members of the family, that were worse for wear, so it didn't seem that bad. I was sat minding my own business when my dad came over and asked me if I was okay.
'I'm fine' I said. 'Just a bit hot' wiping my forehead.

He put his arm on my shoulder and asked if I wanted to go out for some fresh air. I nodded my head and got up with him and headed outside. I was happy just to stand by the door, but he had told me that the barn had horses around the back, so we walked towards the end of the barn. There was no light on the side, so it was dark. As I sat outside on a big log with my dad, he had told me I was a big girl now. I didn't see any horses, but it was clear that my dad wanted to talk to me, so I didn't mention it.

He said he was and I quote 'Sorry for being nasty when I get moody Sarah; daddy loves you.' I told him it was okay, and he replied with.

'Look at me Sarah, daddy is sometimes angry, but it doesn't mean I don't love you. You are my big girl now' he smiled.

I started to relax and smiled back, 'It's okay dad.' He then snapped at me.

'It is daddy, call me daddy. Say it! Say daddy.'

By this point, I had a mild Irish accent, and he told me he liked it when I called him daddy. 'Okay daddy' I snapped back.

Oh, the look he gave me, it was a bit like the evil stare that he would give me usually, but he had a menacing smile at the same time. I closed my eyes and waited to get hit, but instead, he put his arm around me.

'You are lucky I haven't smacked you' he said.

'Tell daddy that you love him, and I will let you off.'

Phew, I thought to myself. 'I love you daddy' I said battering my eyelids.

'Okay,' he smiled, 'Give me a big kiss, and we will forget about it.'

I paused and looked at him confused. Dad never kissed me, or ever showed me any affection, but it was nice to be liked instead of being beaten.

So, I agreed and puckered up my lips. He pulled me closer, so I was almost on his knee, and he places his open palm on my bum and put his lips on mine.
His breath was hot and smelled of cigarettes, and his lips were dry and cracked. I could feel his hand moving on my bum, and I tried to move away, but he just pulled me closer. I wanted to tell him to stop, but he just pressed his face closer to mine. Only then I heard Amy calling my dad's name.

'Jase, it is Laura. Come quickly' she was shouting, but I couldn't see her.

Dad looked at me in disgust and pushed me away so hard I had almost lost my balance.

'What do you think you're playing at' he said as he stood up.

Then he walked away, and I thought I saw him giggling to himself. I just sat on the floor and cried my quiet tears; only I could hear the screams inside my head, I was so confused.

Dad said he hated me so many times, but tonight he told me he loved me, it made out that it should have been a good thing, but I just couldn't get my head around it.

I did as I was told, and he still pushed me away. I didn't know how I felt really, but I did know I didn't like what had just happened, and I didn't want it to happen again, at least being told I was hated and unwanted, I knew where I stood.

Then I started to overthink; I couldn't explain what had just happened.

My dad said sorry for being mean to me, he told me that he loved me, and he kissed me, yes, his lips lingered on mine longer than I had felt comfortable with, but I was his daughter, and I had seen dad's kiss their kids all the time. It was normal, but it still didn't feel right. I started to get angry with myself, and placed my hands either side of my waist, and was gripping hold of the grass so hard that it was stinging my fingertips. The tears were still falling from my snotty nose, and tickling my cheeks as they ran down my face. I was so confused and had such conflicting feelings, I was happy that dad was kind to me but the way he pushed me away when Amy had called him, made me think that this was wrong, but I wasn't even sure why.

Moving Times...

      Not much happened after that New Year's Eve party, dad sometimes got angry over the most stupid of things, like one day I had dropped a cup of the side in the kitchen and split my mum's coffee all over the floor. Dad went mental at me, dragging me by the hair and throwing me onto my bed, a few slaps to the back of my skull, screamed some horrible abuse at me but I had learned to switch off and was thinking about the song I had just heard on the radio moments before. I snapped out of it slightly as he walked towards me again, grabbed my chin, and forced me to look at him. He told me I was a stupid dickhead. He then walked out of my room and slammed my door. It was early in the afternoon, so I hadn't even had my lunch, but I was forbidden from leaving my bedroom, unless I needed the toilet of course. I had been sent to bed without any lunch or dinner, just for spilling a cup of, coffee over. From the argument and shouting downstairs, I guessed mum's coffee had the white powder in it again.

I was almost eight and getting ready for the summer holidays, which I hated because it meant spending most of my time in the house. Life had started to get me down, the consent arguing between my parents, dad kicking off whenever he felt the need to discipline me and the twins had begun ruining all my toys. I would get home from school, and they would have cut my Barbie's hair off or drawn all over my teddies. It seemed like everything I owned; I had to share with my brothers, and anything they owned, I wasn't allowed to touch.

One sunny afternoon, shortly after the cup incident, I was walking home from school, which was only a five-minute walk. As I was started to walk over the bridge just outside the school gates, I notice my aunty Amy stood the other side of the bridge. I was worried something was wrong because no one ever met me from school. For the past year, I had been trusted to go on my own, I think it was just so mum and dad didn't have to get out of bed and take me, but they told me it was because they thought I was big enough. I see other parents collect their children after school, watching the other kids running up to their parents cuddling them and the kids being asked how their day was. I could only wish my parents even cared what I was doing, they never asked, and I never told them how things were at school, what would be the point in ever saying anything. Most of the time I spoke I got told to shut up, I was taught only to talk when someone had spoken to me. As I arrived at the other side of the bridge Amy put her hand out for me to hold, 'Why are you here' I asked her quite blunt.

'You are coming to stay with your aunty Tracey or me for a few weeks' she said 'Your mum and dad are finding you a new house. You will be staying with me until the end of the holidays'.

That was six weeks away I thought to myself. I asked if the twins were at their house and she explained on the walk home, that my mum and dad had moved to Chester in England and that they took the twins but thought it was best to leave me at her house, so I could finish the school year.

As the weeks went on, I had started to relax at my Aunt's house, which meant I had begun to play up a bit. When I was naughty though she would make me stand in the middle of the room with my hands on my head,

'This is better than getting smacked and beaten' I said to her on one occasion, she shouted at me and told me off for saying such nasty things about my parents; I was made to stand there for an extra hour for the cheek of it.

I didn't mind, my arms ached after about half hour, but it was better than getting punched in the ribs or kicked in the shins. That was a good one for my dad; he could argue that most kids my age banged their shins while playing outside, and no one saw my back or my ribs, so it didn't matter how badly bruised I got.

As long as he didn't hit my face, that's all that mattered to him. It was the day before the summer holidays, and Amy had booked my plane tickets weeks before because I was paranoid that my mum and dad had left me there to start a new life without me. I was glad to be going St John's school anyway. No one liked me, and I spent all day on my own, the other kids picked on me because they couldn't understand how my dad was Irish, yet I still had an English accent.

They used to call me a Brit and throw items at me, so I was glad to be leaving. I was packing my things in the blue holdall that belonged to Uncle Paul when suddenly, I noticed Sally standing behind me; she had come to keep an eye on me, just in case I stole her expensive toys. You see, she had these horses which cost her dad a small fortune, and only her and her big sister Vee could play with them. They just were on her shelf catching dust most of the time. I thought it was a little unfair as she never got them down when I was in her room, but she always played with them when her sister was in there with her, maybe she was scared I would break or damage them in some way. To be fair at the same time, she knew that I took a lot of pride the small number of toys that I owned myself, so surely, she should have given me a chance.

That night I couldn't sleep very well, one part of me was excite that I was moving back with my family. The other part of me was scared that the beating would start again, but I had decided that night that as long I was as good as I could be, and as long as I did what mum and dad said it would all be okay. We would all live happily without any arguments or fall out; I had it all understood in my head as I finally drifted off to sleep, that night I had dreamt that I was looking down on the family at the New Year's Eve gathering.

Everything seemed the same as it did when I was at the party six months previously, but I could see my dad sat outside. In my dream I moved closer and could see a young girl with blonde hair sitting beside him, he was kissing her the same way as he kissed me, the man was rubbing his leg up and down and holding on to her bum just like he did with me, then I woke up.

I remember being upset when I woke up, I had tears on my cheeks, and my pillow was soggy, I had guessed I'd be crying a while in my sleep. As I sat up in bed, I had felt quite ill, and my nose was all bunged up from crying. I could feel my mouth filling up with water, and I ran into the bathroom, throwing up all in my hands on the way. I had managed to keep the warm lumpy, sick in my mouth till I got to the bathroom, but the door was locked. I stood outside the door but couldn't hold it in any longer and splattered most of the hallway, what was left of the stew I had eaten the night before. Just then Sally unlocked the bathroom door.

'Ewe you dirty cow' she sniggered.

'Mum' she yelled 'Sarah's been sick all over ya floor' she looked at me and whispered

'You dirty rat, glad you're fucking leaving today.'

I stood on the landing, and just nodded my head in agreement as she pushed past me digging her elbow into my ribs in the process.

'Good fucking ridding's' she said as she slammed her bedroom door behind her.

I locked myself in the bathroom again and cried, I got good at crying silently, tears would stream down my face and drip from my chin, but the only sound that would come out was when I needed to catch my breath, and then you would only hear a tiny whimper if anything.
I did feel ill, but after throwing up and washing my face, I started to get ready for the day ahead.
I remember feeling relief as Amy dropped her kids off, with Uncle Derek, and the nerves didn't kick back in until I saw the sign to the airport.

Aunt Amy was okay with the whole sick incident and guessed it was my nerves because I was going on a plane for the first time, and if that wasn't worrying enough.
I was going on a flight on my own, no adult with me except for the stewardess that would sit at the front of the plane with me.

That wasn't why I was nervous. I was worried that dad would be horrible again, or that mum had got used to me not being around and that maybe she was enjoying life without me. I had so many different thoughts going through my little head that I hadn't noticed us getting to the airport until Amy had parked the car.
She had left me with the stewardess, and I had remembered thinking I was special because everyone was lined up waiting to board, and I was walked straight past them.

I boarded the plane and sat at the very front of the aircraft, right by the window. The stewardess reached behind me and pulled my seatbelt over me, she asked me to lift my feet up, and she pushed a button on the side of my seat. I didn't know what she was doing so I just sat quietly. Then what seemed out of nowhere a table popped out from under my chair and she checked it and secured it to the hook by the window. She then patted me on the head

'Do you need anything sweet?' she asked.

I shook my head and smiled at her. I was scared stiff, but she soon put me at ease, I think it must have been written all over my face, she sat down beside me and started asking what treats I like and what my favorite drink was.

She then said, 'we will see what we can do, only the best for our VIP guest' she winked at me and got up of the chair.

I didn't know what she meant, so when she returned I had asked her what VIP meant when she told me I was a very important passenger.
I smiled so hard it hurt my face, I was happy she said this to me, and wished she was my mum.
I couldn't remember the last time anyone had been kind to me, well that's a lie, I relived the New Year's Eve like it was yesterday, and it wasn't the nice, that I wanted ever again.

The stewardess must have seen the confusion in my eyes, but she took my mind off this train of thought, when she showed me what was in her bag, she had whole loads of treats, curly wurly's and chomps, Quavers.
She had found orange juice for me and had a coloring book and a set of crayons.

This lady was very nice, and I thought she was only friendly because she felt sorry for me, which I didn't mind if this was how she was treating me. I felt very special on the plane journey that I had almost forgotten I was up thousands of feet in the air.

Once we had arrived at Manchester airport, I was told to stay seated until everyone had got off the plane and then the stewardess explained she would walk me to where my parents would be waiting to collect me. By this point, I knew her by actual name, Louise, which I couldn't forget as that was my middle name. I hadn't eaten all my treats because the journey had only taken forty minutes, so I left them on the table when I packed my things back away in my bag.

'No, you can keep them' she said.

'Thank you, Louise,' I replied with a smile.

We made our way to the door and got off the plane. I was waiting at the arrivals desk like planned. My mum came to collect me, but she was over an hour late, and Louise had to leave me with another lady, as she needed to re-board the plane to get back to Belfast.
The new lady wasn't as friendly, and we sat in science for about forty-five minutes while we waited for me to be collected.

After mum had met me, we had a ten-minute walk to the bus station; she was apparently in a rush as she dragged me by the arm the whole way there. I told her I could jog if she let go of me.

'You know what happened last time we had a jog.' and with that, she dragged me that little bit rougher.

As we approached the bus station there were a few people already waiting; mum said we were lucky we didn't miss the bus as I was walking far too slowly for her liking.

While we were waiting, she explained that the sister Kath had moved to Manchester, while we were in Belfast. I knew my aunt Kath from when we lived with Nan in Crosby. She was Katie's mother, but I hadn't seen her for years. Mum was explaining everything and went on to tell me how Kath had moved to a new house and left her, dad and the twins homeless, and they were staying with friends of Kath's called Craig and Jackie who they had met during the weeks I was still in Belfast. When we got to Craig's house, mum said I had to be good and that dad was out finding us a place to stay but would be home soon enough, just the mention of his name has me knowing I will be good as gold. It was like she was warning me not to make a peek around him.

I met Jackie and Craig, and I thought they seemed nice, they had a son called Simon, who was about my age. He had asked me if I want to play in the back garden with him and the twins, but I was tired and just wanted to sit down, my feet were aching, and my head was starting to hurt, it was no offense to the boy, I just didn't feel up to it.

'Suit yourself; I won't be asking you again.'

He kept his promise too. I spent the next week just watching TV, and playing board games with Jackie, she was fun, like a big kid at heart and she was very polite and had such a gentle voice.

By the end of the week, dad had found us a rented house on a council estate just twenty minutes away, and he had seemed happy and relaxed on the day we finally moved out of Craig's. Dad had promised to keep in touch with them, and Jackie had vowed to buy some jigsaws at the weekend so that we could do together a week later, but I was never to see Craig and Jackie again after that day.

Our New Home...

We moved into our new house, in Rusty Gardens, Chester, it was a lovely enough street, but I did think it amusing when I told anyone I lived at number four Rusty Gardens. I was sent to a school almost thirty minutes away, which seemed weird to me because our house was right next door to a primary school. The side of our house backed onto the school field, it would have been so easy to jump over the fence and stroll into class, but dad had insisted that I was to go to a Catholic school, so I was sent, to Saint John Fisher Catholic Primary.

The school was small, but it was very well looked after, and I met some good friends. I remember always being in a big gang of girls, and I had become popular because I was quick at doing fish braids, I started charging some kids 30p per braid, and that was my first glimpse into making my own money. I was only nine years old and never really got pocket money, so this was all new to me, when one of the girls said it would be a smart idea to make some money, we all decided to try it out. I had been asked to teach a few other girls, so they had a chance of making money too. I loved school, and I was like a sponge, always thirsty for knowledge. I had always enjoyed learning new things and some of the other girls, who I never really spoken to, had started to resent me.

I liked the attention I was getting from the teachers, but the girls didn't, so they started calling me names. Teacher's pet was the kindest name they had for me, but it was funny because they all still wanted me to help them out with different money-making ideas at lunchtimes. I didn't like them, and I let them tease me. I think I just wanted to be accepted, for a change.

I did do a stupid thing one day, after getting a good hiding, because the twins had wound my dad up, I decided I needed money to get away. I saw my mother's ring on the sink in the bathroom that morning, and I had hoped I would be able to sell it in school. My young, inexperienced head believed I could sell the ring for loads of money and get a train to anywhere that wasn't my home. My plan didn't work out at all, as my teacher had noticed me messing with the ring in class. She took it from me and said she would be ringing my parents and telling them all about it in the process. Luckily for me, it was my mum who answered the phone call, and after nothing being said by my father, I had guessed my mum hadn't told him.

Apart from that one stupid mistake, school life overall was good; it's a pity the same couldn't be said, at home. My mum and dad had started to take tablets now to get them high; they were always off, their faces. I was getting older, and I could tell whenever they had taken drugs or not. I had overheard enough conversations to know the names of the drugs and kind of what people took them for; dad made mum take them, so she would have a better sex drive. I didn't know what that meant, but I knew the word sex was rude, this was just a saying dad had used time and again when they argued about it.

Dad would call mum a 'frigid bitch' and always accused her of having an affair. I didn't understand what that meant either.

I regularly saw my dad hitting my mum, but never as much as he would hit me. I started to believe that he hated me.

I heard him always say to mum that he couldn't stand me and can't help but lose his temper with me, but I didn't understand why it had to be me, and what I had done so terribly wrong to make him hate me this way. This is a question I still don't know the answer to, and I am unsure I ever will.

It was spring term, and I was stuck at home with dad and the twins, I remember kneeling on the couch, looking out of the living room at all the kids playing outside in the sun. I had to stay in because dad was upstairs busy, and I was needed to look after the twins; Mum was at work, she was working as a cleaner for a hotel in the center of town a few miles away, dad didn't seem to mind because mum was earning a good wage.

She must have been getting generous tips because dad would say she had been a good girl if she came home with more than a set amount. The twins had both fallen asleep while watching some stupid baby cartoon that mum played on the video player repeatedly. I decided that I wasn't needed to watch the twins because they were asleep, so I went upstairs to find my dad and ask if I could play out the front. I walked into his bedroom, but he wasn't in there, you could see that he had been sat in bed reading his big boy magazines because they were all over the floor with the duvet half on and off his bed. Then I heard him cough from behind me. As I turned around I seen the bathroom door was closed and it was only closed if someone was in there, so I knocked on the door.

'Dad' I shouted, but I had no reply, I knew sometimes he ignored me if I didn't say his name correctly, so I yelled again louder.
'Daddy, can I go out and play, the twin is asleep?' He shouted back that he couldn't hear me, so I repeated myself even louder.

'I still can't hear you for fuck sake' came from the other side of the bathroom door, then I heard the door unlock.

I stood there waiting for him to come out of the bathroom, but he didn't, so I leaned towards the door.
'Daddy, the twins are asleep, can I play out?'

'Come here, I can't fucking, hear you!' he replied.

I pulled the handle down and as I walked in the room. I saw my dad stood in the middle of the bathtub with no clothes on. Like he was getting ready to have a bath, but the taps were off, and there was no water in the tub. I felt awkward, and dad didn't say anything he just smiled at me. I told him I was sorry and went to walk away, but he called me back, and I knew by now that he liked nothing more than to hit me if I didn't listen, so, I turned back around and looked at the floor.

He shouted, 'so what is so god damn important,'

I still had my eyes on the floor, and I replied, 'Can I play outside please?' with that he stepped out if the bath and walked towards me.

I could see his feet getting closer, and I closed my eyes and flinched my arm up to my face. I thought he was going to whack me, but he just stood there.

'Where are the twins?' he asked.

I told him they were on the sofa both asleep; he had said to me that I was to stay in for the afternoon and if I was well behaved, I could go out later when mum got home, we had a whole five-minute conversation.

I didn't know where to look, and I felt uncomfortable, while he stood there with no clothes on, and to make it worse, he didn't try and cover anything up. He was standing just over a foot away from me smiling with that creepy grin, and stark bollock naked. I had wondered to myself whether or not he had taken drugs, but I daren't ask him so I would never know.

After the awkwardness of the few seconds silence he giggled and patted my head, he then he sent me to my bedroom. As I sat on the end of my bed I started to well up with tears; I didn't care about not going out to play. I was used to being stuck in the house all the time anyway, so that didn't bother me, but I cried because I was so confused, a thousand thoughts went through my mind at once, and I didn't understand anything that had just happened.

A few days had passed, and nothing was said, about me seeing dad with no clothes on and that's the way I liked it, I was so embarrassed.

I thought maybe my dad was also, and that's why he hadn't said anything to my mum. It was about six in the evening and mum was getting ready for work, her shift started at seven, but she needed to leave earlier so she could get to work on time.
The twins were both fast asleep in bed, and I had just got my nightdress on ready to say goodnight to my mum before just she left for work.

Usually, dad would send me straight up to bed when mum had gone out but for some reason, this time was different.

Dad ushered me into the living room and told me to sit on the sofa. I was sure he was going to tell me off, but instead, he sat beside me and pulled me by the top of my arm towards him, I was scared and didn't say a word for fear of getting hit, so, I sat ridged beside him.

'Relax for fuck sake' dad snapped and pulled my body closer to him in a cuddling position.

He put my hand on his leg, and I moved it away instinctively.

'Just fucking relax and sit, the way I tell you to do' he said slowly and calmly.

I looked up at him, feeling him warm smelly breath on my face and I could see the evil shine in his eyes again. His cold stare sent shivers down my spine, and I buried my head under his armpit in the hope that if I couldn't see him looking at me, I could try and imagine I was far, far away from him.

I was trying so hard to believe I was somewhere safe; I imagined I was at my nan's house and I could feel a smile start to form on my face until the reality of the situation dawned on me.

I felt my dad's open hand wrap around my exposed bum cheek, and I could feel him cherishing my bum, digging his fingers harder and harder into my skin. It hurt but I felt paralyzed to say anything, I silently cried inside and just tried to ignore what was happening.

He took hold of my hand and placed in on the couch of his jeans. Slowly pushed my hand up and down, digging his fingers into the top of my hand to make me move in the way he wanted.

I could feel a strange hardness inside his jeans, and I guessed it was his manhood. I moved my hand out of the way, but he took his hand off my bum and wrapped his fingers around my hair and pulled so tight I thought he had ripped my hair out, I squealed in pain, as he pulled my face up to his. Still with a firm grasp on my hair he whispered.

'Just shut up, and fucking enjoy it you dirty bitch.'
I tried to speak, but he pulled my hair tighter around his hand and scowled 'you will learn to love it, or I will make your life hell. Do you understand?' he asked.

I nodded my head, and he placed my hand firmly back on his jeans and forced me to rub him. His penis was getting very hard he told me he had to get more comfortable and started to unzip his jeans. He pulled it out and told me to hold it; I placed my hand on the top of it. I turned away as he took it out and he ordered me to look at him, as I turned to look it was sticking right out of his trousers and was all shiny and red.

'Hold it' he said so I placed the palm of my hand on the top of it.

'Not like that' he snapped, and he placed my fingers on it and showed me how the slide my hand up and down.

I felt sick, and I think he could tell because I was heaving, instead of stopping, he just smiled at me and said,

'This is lesson one; you wait till I show you the best bits, then you will fucking heave, you dirty little tart, you can tell you are your mother's daughter.'

My arm was getting tired, and I wanted to just go to bed, it felt like I had been rubbing his penis for hours, but I glanced at the clock and mum had only been out of the house for forty-five minutes.

My dad rested his head on the back of the sofa while I continued to do as he said,

'Don't stop, please don't stop.'

He placed his hand on top of mine, squeezing my hand tighter around him, moving our hands fast, up and down, up and down, faster and faster. His head fell backward again, and he made the strangest grunting sound I had ever heard, then I noticed a warm sticky cream all over my hands.

'Oh, that is what daddy needed' he said sounding out of breath, he released my hands and pushed me off the sofa onto the floor.

'Now wash your hands, you dirty, dirty little slag and then get your fucking arse into bed' he shouted.

I got up and ran straight into the bathroom. I closed the door and sat behind it, tears rolling down my cheeks while I was staring down at my dirty hand. I washed my hand and climbed into bed, confused and scared, I sobbed myself to sleep and was hoping that what just happened was just a bad nightmare, but I knew it wasn't and as I lay there falling asleep I remember dreading the next day when I would have to face him again. I was so worried I felt like I couldn't breathe and thinking that I was happy enough not ever to wake up the next morning.

Daddy's Girl...

Over the next few months, my father's behavior towards me got more and more erratic. I had celebrated my ninth birthday, which was nothing special. I didn't feel like I even had a birthday, everything was the same except, mum had brought me a few new toys, which the twins were told to play with to keep them entertained. Even on my birthday, he had found a reason to start on me. He would seem to make up reasons to smack me, especially in front of my mum. He would come up with some excuse like two pounds had gone missing from his wallet, which was impossible because it was always in the back pocket of his jeans, so even if I did want to steal from him, I never could. Mum still believed him and took his side no matter what the reason was, even if it was something simple like my bedroom was messy. She would get so sick and tired of listening to him tell me off that she would use it as an excuse to go out, which suited dad down to the ground. Once I was on my own with him, he could do what he wanted.

It was on a warm afternoon in July, that dad had talked mum into taking the twins out for the day, we were all planned to go out as a family, but dad had said that because I had wet the bed, I wasn't allowed to go with them.

I was to stay at home with him as a punishment for being nine years old and still wetting the bed, I didn't even wet the bed, but mum had to believe I had, and there was nothing I could do about it.

What happened that morning was worse than any bed wetting!

My dad had come into my room in the early hours and sat at the bottom of my bed, I woke up, and he told me to go back to sleep as he sat there in the dark. I closed my eyes and faced the wall, but I could feel the bed shaking, so, I sat up again. My dad was wanking himself off, while sat there.

'Go to fucking sleep' he said when he noticed me looking at him, so, I turned back around feeling confused and scared.

Any other time he had his penis out he made me rub it till he made a mess but this time he just wanted to masturbate on my bed while I pretended to be asleep. I felt him stand up, I could still hear the sticky sound of him pleasing himself, and I felt him lift my covers off me. I lay there cold, too scared to move. All I had on was a vest and a pair of knickers, as I lay there shivering I felt the warm sticky stuff drip over my thighs, I tried to move, but my dad started to rub it into my skin.

'Don't fucking move?' He said. I tried my hardest just to ignore him, and after a few minutes, he walked out of my bedroom. He returned with a glass of warm water and a flannel and washed me; I kept my eyes firmly closed, the water was dripping down my legs, onto my mattress. When he had finished, he kissed me on the top of my head and put my covers back on top of me, and then casually, walked back out of my room closing my door behind him.

I was soaked, my duvet was dripping wet too, as I lay there waiting for the morning to come, feeling far too scared to move.

I heard my mum wake up first; she seemed to be in a good mood as she walked into the twin's room,
'Good morning my babies' she said as she opened their curtains.

By now they were almost five and acted like little brats, mum was forever shouting at them, and they didn't take any notice of her. Today was the day, that dad had planned for us to go out for the day. My mother was happy, that was until she came into my room to wake me up. As she walked in, she must have seen my bed was soaking wet; she started shouting abuse uncontrollably at me, telling me I was a 'dirty tramp.'

Even if I wanted to say anything I didn't have the chance, dad walked in behind her and told her he would deal with me. I knew what was coming as my mum walked out of the door closing it behind her. He walked over and started slapping me on the back of my head. I made the mistake of telling him that he did this to me but soon regretted answering back. He grabbed my face a pushed his thumb under my chin and pulled me up, off my bed; I thought he was going to break my neck. He pushed me to the floor, digging his knee into my side; he then lent down and put his face close to mine.

'It was you, all fucking you. You make me do these things to you, you dirty bitch and if I ever hear you talk about it to anyone, and I mean anyone, I will kill you. Do you understand?' His voice was low but just as intimidating.

'Yes' I replied.

He then stood up and pulled me to my feet by my arm. As I stood vulnerable in front of him, he placed his hand under my chin and lifted my face to look at him.

'I only treat you like this because you are your mother's daughter. You only have yourself to blame. You look like her you know, and if she can't give me what I want, you will' he smiled and walked towards my door.

'Now clean up your mess Sarah Louise and don't make me tell you again' and he walked away leaving me on my own with a hundred thoughts swimming around my little head.

While dad helped mum to get the twins ready for the day out, the day out that I was meant to enjoy too, I was upstairs crying to myself in the shower. I felt so dirty, confused and scared and as I stood there with water running down my back I couldn't help but relive the night before, the water reminded me that my father had made that mess all over me. I was ten years old, but I knew this wasn't normal behavior, and as I stood there washing with my pink Disney princess sponge, I felt sick and dizzy, and I tried my hardest to put the thoughts to the back of my mind. I got out of the shower and got dressed because I needed the toilet, the toilet was separate to our bathroom, it was tiny and didn't even have a sink in there, the room itself, was less than four square foot. I walked out of the bathroom but my dad was stood on the top of the stairs as if he was waiting to use the sink, I walked past him into the toilet, when I was finished I stepped back onto the landing, and he was still stood there waiting.

I looked at him confused, and he said, 'Just you and me now, love.'

That sent shivers down my spine. I knew that nothing I could say or do would change what I had already known, and what I was about to experience.

Lesson Two...

So, mum was out for the day, and my dad had managed to convince her that he would be okay at home looking after me and that he didn't mind missing out, just as long as it stopped me wetting the bed again. He told her that it was a lesson I needed to learn, if only I knew that, that comment had, a different meaning once she had left the house. I was in my bedroom playing with my Barbie's, and my dad had been acting weird all morning since my mum had gone out, like the standing on the landing staring at me with cold evil eyes. It was about eleven o clock in the morning, and he had walked into my room, he said he had something to show me and ushered me to the landing, I put my toys down and went with him. He told me to go to the toilet.

'But I don't need it' I said,

'I don't care just get in there now' he shouted.

So, I did as I was told and went and stood inside the tiny toilet. I guessed my dad was going to make me clean it or something.

'Time for lesson two' he said walking towards me.

I looked at him confused, and he said 'You have mastered number one, you dirty little slut. Now let me see how long it takes you to, master this one' he said rubbing his penis.

'Shhh, this protest is killing the mood' he replied, and with that he wrapped, his hands around my neck and pulled me to my feet.

I couldn't breathe and could feel his hands getting tighter and tighter, but I didn't care anymore. It didn't matter if I died. No one would miss me. Then he let go, and I fell onto the toilet seat, I couldn't have landed anywhere else. The walls were either side of me, and my dad was standing in the only floor space there was in this tiny room, with his back to the locked door. I had nowhere to escape.

'Get up bitch, sit straight.' He repeated himself about five times before I finally moved and sat as he commanded.

He made it very clear to me that I was to do exactly, what he had told me to do, and if I didn't listen to him, then he would enjoy beating me till I begged for his cock in my mouth. If I had any sense, it was best just do what he said. So, I agreed with him. After a few minutes of him trying to force my mouth open more, he gave up and told me to do mouth exercises to make it easier next time. He showed me how. Like I didn't know how to open my mouth, I knew how to do it but I couldn't see how trying to force my mouth open with my fingers would make much difference but I knew I had to do what he said.

So, I sat on my bed and practicing how to open my mouth wider. I cried uncontrollably, snot running all down my hands but I kept trying, I was scared that if his penis didn't fit in my mouth next time, I would be in severe trouble, and I had no idea when next time would be.

Next time would turn out to be a few weeks later.

I had been sexually abused for over a year now, and it sounds stupid, but I had started to get used to it, I knew that if I just did as I was told it would be over quicker.

The more I struggled, the worse it got for me, so I took the easy route. Mum had gone to bingo with some friends from work, and the twins were in bed. I was sat in the living room when I got called upstairs.

'Bedtime Sarah' my dad shouted. So, I turned the television off and put my glass of milk on the side in the kitchen; I was walking towards the stairs when my dad shouted downstairs for me to hurry up. As I ran up the stairs, he was standing on the landing, and he pointed me into his room.

'Sit on the bed' he said calmly 'Your mother has been very disappointing lately, so I was hoping you could help me out' he said.

I knew what that meant, either he wanted me to wank him off or try and put it in my mouth again. I looked at him hoping he could see the tears build up in my eyes but he didn't look at me as he took his jeans off and placed them on the floor.

'Your mum won't be back for hours' he whispered as he lent down and kissed me on the cheek.

I turned my head away, and he told me to stop being moody. Stop being moody! can you believe the cheek of him, I was almost eleven years old, and I was doing things to my dad that my mum had been doing 'disappointedly lately.' I thought that if she were doing these sick things to him properly, then I wouldn't have to do them to him, so the resentment towards her started from that point on.

Dad had decided if he put it in my mouth before it got too hard that it would be easier for me, so he rubbed his penis across my lips and told me to lick the end of it. I thought I was going to throw up, but I did what he had said and started to lick the end of it like it was a banana, which is the name he gave it. He then put both of his hands around the back of my head and pulled my slightly open mouth towards him.

'Suck it you dirty bitch' he scowled. 'Suck it like a banana' he said over and over again.

So, I opened my mouth and let him put it inside. I was hoping my daddy had seen how much I had practiced opening my mouth, and he did. My dad pushed his penis deeper into my mouth, and I started to heave. Water was building up in my mouth, and I thought I was about to throw up all over him, but he kept pushing deeper and deeper. Tears were running down my cheeks I could hardly breathe and was sure I was going to be sick. Then he released my head and let me move out of the way. I scurried across the bed to get away from him. He looked at me as he grabbed his jeans off the floor and said

'Sorry.'

I sat on his bed a curled up in a ball crying; he must have gone downstairs because the next thing I knew my mum was carrying me into my bed

Hospital Dash...

It was the summer holidays; I had not long had my eleventh birthday, my dad's new thing to do to me was make me read articles from his dirty magazines, they were full of pictures of naked couples having oral sex with each other. He must have got this new idea for lesson number three from me reading my books to the twins at night; this was my new job because mum was always out, which gave dad more time to train me up as he would call it. Not only would I have to read this dirty stuff about words I didn't understand like 'cum' and 'pussy's' I had to do it completely naked, with no clothes on at all. Lying on my front with my legs open while my dad played with his penis starting at my eleven-year-old private parts. I hated every minute of it, but I just keep reading and trying to not notice his evil glint in his eye and that false twisted smile.

As I was reading through the pages, I got to a page where a man was licking the girl's bits, and it went into graphic detail on how to do it. Dad said that gave him an idea. He turned me around on the bed and had my legs open, with my feet dangling towards the floor, he pulled me down the bed so that my bum on the foot of the bed and I froze. He knelt in between my legs; he was kissing my belly, then, I felt his hand slowly creeping up my leg. I moved my leg out of the way, and he started kissing me lower, just below my belly button. His hand had moved towards my vagina, and as he started rubbing me I begged him to stop, but he said it was my turn to be the teacher. He said I had read all about it and that I needed to know what they were talking about. He continued to kiss my belly and rubbing me below, my legs started to shake, I felt my body going stiff, and I felt a sharp pain in between my legs as he tried to push his finger inside me. I cried out in pain, it was like a knife had been placed there; he moved his finger away.

He told me 'not to cry' and that he would 'kiss it all better.'

He started kissing me as it showed in the magazine that I had been made to read. I tried with all my strength to move out of the way, but he had pinned me down with his arms around my thighs so tight that I couldn't even move an inch. It seems the more I struggled, the more determined he was to continue, so I lay there and just tried to block out what was happening to me.

When he had finally finished he ordered me to get dressed and get out of his sight, so I grabbed my clothes off the bed and tried to stand up, but my legs felt weak, and I almost fell to the floor. I sat on the edge of the bed crying, and he walked over to me, calling me a stupid bitch and started beating me around the back of my head with his fists. Punching me harder and harder, until I fell to the ground.

'Don't you fucking cry' was all he kept saying as a harder bang to the head came until I blacked out.

He must have moved me while I was out cold because when I woke up, I was half dressed and lying on the top of my bed. I must have whimpered or something as I came around because as soon as I opened my eyes, he was stood in the doorway.

'You're awake then.' He said.

I nodded my head, but my neck hurt.

'Serves you right for crying like a baby' he replied, and with that, he walked out of my room again.

I lay there in pain, confused and hurting, wondering why dad was so nasty to me. I was scared to fall asleep in case he beat me again because he had seemed angry that I had passed out on him. I didn't see him again for the rest of that evening.

I had woken in the middle of the night to go to the toilet, and as I tried to walk to the bathroom I ached all over, my head really hurt. I turned on the toilet light, pulled my knickers down and sat on the toilet seat, still half asleep. I was shocked as I looked down at the floor I saw big red marks on the tops of both of my thighs when dad had pinned me down. I ran into my bedroom and didn't even wash my hands first before running straight into my room and climbing under my covers. I lay there that night wide awake, tears ran down the side of my face, dripping into my ears. I was getting really frustrated as I wiped the wet dampness from my eyes. I curled myself up into a ball, facing the door, I always felt safer if I could see my bedroom door, and still do to this day. I was laying on my side shaking and sniffling. I don't think I had ever felt so angry in my life, but I was more so, mad at myself for letting this happen. I closed my eyes tightly, frustrated and annoyed with myself for crying; I would cry myself to sleep yet again. I knew for a fact that night, I was trapped, with this monster I am told to call my daddy.

The next morning, I woke up, I had been sweating while I was asleep, and my nighty was stuck to my back, as I tried to move I felt the most painful shooting pains I had ever experienced all through my body. I couldn't breathe, as the burning pain in my lower stomach started to get more intense, I lay there scared that I was dying.

I was in severe pain, but I couldn't shout out, and when I tried to get help, no sound came out of me. I looked down at my belly where I guessed the pain was coming from and I could see a massive red lump in the groin of my leg; I thought I had broken my bone or something, I started to panic. That just made me struggle to breathe again, I felt dizzy and sure that I was about to die, but I didn't mind. I was ready to leave.

I must have passed out again because the next thing I remember was being in a wheelchair at the local hospital. As I came around, the lights were blinding, so I closed my eyes tight again, I could hear my mum and dad were near me, from the sound of their voices but I didn't want to open my eyes and didn't want them to know I was awake. I could hear them arguing, my dad kept repeating that it was his fault, mum didn't seem to understand what he was rabbling on about, but I did. I wondered if he had broken me while he was kissing me better the night before, but I didn't say anything, I couldn't even if I tried, the pain was still there, but at least I could breathe now.

I remember thinking to myself that if I wasn't dead then maybe I was meant to be here, perhaps I am alive because God has some purpose for me. I wasn't particularly religious, but I had been attending Catholic schools, and some of the teachings had worn off on me. As I sat in the wheelchair, I heard a young lady talking, when my mum replied I realized they were talking about me.

I opened my eyes and seen a young nurse, she looked younger than my mum anyway, but she had an anxious look on her pretty face, and her eyes were sad. I remember wondering why she was upset but I knew I wouldn't ask her. The nurse saw me look at her, and asked me if I knew my name, 'Sarah' I said quietly,

'We need to give you an x-ray, to see why you are in pain, can you stand up?' she asked.

I shook my head knowing I was in too much pain to move, so she bent down and place one arm around my back and the other under my knees, and scooped me up into her arms, the pain shot through me like a sharp knife, as she pulled me closer to her. I felt my mouth fill with water, and I threw up all over this poor woman.
I thought she was going to shout at me, but she didn't seem to mind at all and said it was all part of the job.

She carried me into the x-ray room while my mum and dad stayed outside with the twins, who were fast asleep in their pushchair. The nurse lay me down on a bed and put the covers over my legs to keep me warm. She explained that I had been administrated pain relief and that it would start to work soon, she was so caring and kind towards me, I thought about telling her about what my dad had done to me, but I was scared. After all, he was standing the other side of the x-ray door and I believed he would kill me, no matter where I was, so I said nothing as she walked behind the booth where she took x-rays of my insides to see what was happening to me. She took the pictures and walked out of the room, confirming to me that she would be back in a few minutes.

When she returned she had explained that I needed an operation, to remove the lump in the groin of my leg, she told me I would be in the hospital for at least a week, I should have been worried or scared, but I fell of relief washed over me.

I was glad to get a rest from my life at home, as I lay there waiting to be moved into the next available bed.

I tried to imagine what was wrong with me and I couldn't help but wonder what made my dad confess to my mum, that it was his fault. I wondered if he would tell her what had happened, and I was worried she would dislike me even more. My mum was never really the motherly type of parent anyway but if she knew what dad did when she was out. She would probably hate me and want me out of her life, well that's what dad had always told me.

He said that he would have to kill me because if I lived, I would be a reminder to her that I did to him, all the things that she couldn't. He said it wasn't fair and even started to threaten me that he would tell her if I refused to do what he had told me to do.

I believed him, and as much as I hated living at home, it was all I had ever known.

I had only been waiting in my hospital bed for about an hour when a doctor came into my room and told me I had to get ready for surgery; he said my parents had gone home, but my mum would be back in time for me going into theatre.

The pain was getting too much by this point, and I just wanted to get it over and done with, I didn't know what was wrong with me, but it sounded serious the way the doctors kept checking me over.

The small Indian doctor started with putting an armband around the top of my arm; he said it was to check my blood pressure, but I didn't understand what he meant.

'Is that okay?' He asked as he strapped the band to my arm.

I nodded and then the armband filled with air, squeezing my arm tighter.

Once that had finished he would shine a light into my eyes and put a thermometer in my mouth, he did this four times in the space of an hour and a half, while we waited for my mum to arrive.

It seemed like my mum was only in my room for a few minutes when the doctor who was keeping an eye on me and the nurse who did my x-ray for me earlier on in the morning, walked into my room and asked if I was ready to go. I looked up at my mum, and she was crying.
She kissed me on my head and told me that she would be waiting in my room till I got back and that I was very brave. She told me for the first time in my life that she was proud of me and that she loved me.
I smiled as the doctor and nurse wheeled my bed out of the room. When we got outside the operating theatre the doctor asked me if I was feeling okay, stupid question really, I was in agony, the pain was like a burning fire building up inside me trying to push itself through my skin, I was far from alright, but I just nodded my head. He stroked my hair and said it would all be over soon.

I was then, wheeled into a bright white room where three other doctors where waiting for me. The doctor stood to the side of me, held my hand and warned me that I would feel a small sharp scratch on my hand as the put the needle in my hand. I didn't even notice, I just remember feeling sick, and the room started to go dizzy. The general anesthetic had started to work straight away.

When I came around I was back in the room; mum was there sat on the chair beside my best reading her 'women's own' magazine. She noticed me waking up, and she told me she needed to get the doctor, he had told her to get him as soon as I woke up.

Mum walked back to my room a few minutes later and sat on the end of my bed, I was still in pain, but more tender than the burning pain I felt before. I looked under my cover and moved the paper night dress that they must have put on me while I was in surgery, I had a big white plaster across my stomach and blood stains on the tops of my legs.

'What was wrong with me?' I asked my mum.

She explained that part of my intestines had got trapped and the blood circulation was cut to the rest of my body, she called it a strangulated hernia and said I was fortunate that the doctors found it on time.

My mother made it sound severe and dramatic. I could have died I thought to myself. I spent the rest of the week in that room, but it was peaceful, and I felt safe for the first time in a very long time. Dad didn't visit me which was a welcome break, but mum was there every day making sure I was okay and bringing me clean clothes, she seemed different without dad leaning over her shoulder, more attentive and caring.

I wanted to talk to her and tell her what had happened, but I didn't want her to worry, or for dad to have a reason to beat us, so I kept my mouth shut and just enjoyed the time mum and I was getting.

As the week was coming to an end I remember worrying about returning home, I couldn't move very fast and struggled to get up and the fear of dad making me do mums jobs for him petrified me. Knowing full well that I was too weak to fight him off. I hoped that if he saw his eleven-year-old daughter in so much pain, might have made him realize that what he had done was wrong and maybe he could just love me like a proper dad was meant to love their daughter.

I didn't like the way he loved me but also wondered if most dads loved their little girls the way I was loved. Maybe that's why we were born, perhaps that why dads, had little girls so that they could do the jobs that our mothers refused to do. Now I know how stupid that statement sounded.

When we did return home, it wasn't what I had expected at all. Dad had moved the living room around and put my mattress on the floor in there, so I didn't have to climb up the stairs every day. It had been a week since my operation, but I still struggled to walk. The scaring was so close to the groin of my leg that I worried I would split the wound back open if I moved too much, so I was grateful when I had seen my bed made up on the floor.

As I climbed under my covers, dad had come down the stairs with a massive teddy for me, it was a big white bear with a yellow bow on its head, and it was fluffy and soft. The teddy itself must have been the size of me, and I guessed it had cost mum and dad a lot of money at the time. I thanked them and lay my head down. I think all the medicine they had given me, had made me tired and I spent most of my time asleep over the next week or so.

Within a few weeks, I was back to my usual self and well enough to start my new school at the end of the holidays. I was glad to get back to school but was a little worried about going into secondary school, even if I was pleased to be leaving Saint John Fisher the thought of big school scared me a little.

I did have a lot of friends in Saint John's, but the boys were always really mean to me, especially one lad called Keith, he was mean to most girls but seemed to take an extra dislike to me. The horrible boy would spit in my face and call me similar names to the ones my dad called me.

So, for me starting a new school after six weeks holiday, I saw it as a fresh start. My dad had seemed okay with me since I came home from the hospital, so things were looking up, or so I thought they were.

School Drama...

It was the start of October, I had been in my school for about four weeks, in that time I hadn't made many friends, I was the smallest and youngest in my year, I found it hard to talk to all these new people. The girls who used to hang around with me at primary school had new best mates that they had met during the summer holidays so weren't all that interested in talking to me anymore. Even my fish plaits were a thing of the past. I would spend most of my lunch time just sat on the wall outside the canteen, watching all the other kids messing about and chatting with one another. I could hear them all planning to meet up after school, and at the weekends. I was jealous, my mum and dad would never let my mates come home after school, and there was no way I would be allowed to go out to meet them at the weekends. I was very rarely even allowed to play out the front of my house, never mind meet uptown like the girls were all planning.

One girl must have noticed me listening to their conversation and walked towards me.

'What ya looking at ya lickle rat?' she sneered,

'Nothing' I sounded sheepish as my voice cracked.

'Fancy coming out on the rob with us after school?' she asked pointing to her friend stood behind her.

'I'm not allowed' I replied.

The girl started laughing with her friends.
'Oh, bless ya poor lickle girl has to run home to mummy and daddy.'

The rest of the girls were taunting me now and were getting a kick out of upsetting me. I felt stupid when they walked away and had wished I'd said something cooler like not today girls, or maybe next time. I was annoyed with myself for saying 'I wasn't allowed' it made me look like a proper baby. As I sat there with my head in my hands, tears rolling down my cheeks, I was utterly alone in the full playground. Even though everyone was around me, I had taken myself off into my little world, in my mind. I wished the floor would tear open and swallow me whole. I had never felt so stupid. My father did an excellent job at making me feel like shit, but now it was happening at school and home, and I could just tell that this was the start of my school life becoming just as tragic as my life at home.

While I was younger, the school was my great escape, but soon enough I would dread class, just as much as I dreaded going home at quarter past three every day. The gang of girls started to tease me daily, calling me names, telling me I was a daddy's girl, and they would just generally pick on me for not being as streetwise as some of the other kids. I knew I was different, but I started to worry that with the name calling and consent knock to my self-esteem, I must have acted differently too. By the time I was eleven, I knew what my dad was doing to me at home was wrong, but it wasn't till half way through my first term at school I clicked on how bad it all was.

We were sat in class doing sex education when I first realized how bad my situation had got. I was near the back of the classroom sat beside my only friend, June.

As the lesson started most of the girls were all giggly, about the prospect of seeing naked men and women on the nudist video. We had been made to watch it, as part of the birds and bees story. Everyone seemed to be in fits of laughter throughout the ten min programme, but June and I just sat at the back commenting on how childish they all looked.

June had older brothers and had seen them with lack of clothes on many occasions while they were in the toilet or bathroom, she was down to earth and said it didn't bother her, as it was natural. I just listened as she babbled on, and couldn't help but wonder if it was natural for a dad to be doing the things he did to me, then panic set in as the teacher started to tell us about the difference between oral sex and full intercourse.

I felt like I had a massive beacon on my head and I began to get hot, it was right at that exacted moment that I realized the things my dad was making me do was sick, and very, very wrong indeed. I knew it was a secret for a reason, but I thought that it was a secret, to not hurt my mother's feelings, now I realized just the severity of it all. Our teacher finished the lesson with a round of questions, to gauge how much of the lesson we had taken in. I was dreading her getting to my turn, but luckily the back row didn't have the opportunity to answer before the break time bell went off.

As we all rushed to get out of the classroom, the ringleader of the gang stopped and looked directly at me. Julie her name was, and she was the main girl in the group who had been teasing me the most, she was taller than me with long blonde hair and bright blue eyes, I think her good looks made her popular because it couldn't have been her dim-witted personality that's for sure.

She walked towards me and pushed my shoulder; she said she heard me sniggering with June and that she would be waiting for me after school, I knew what she meant and worried I was about to get a beating for no reason. I could have argued back but that wasn't my style, and I had hoped that if she would see that I wasn't mouthy, then maybe she would let me off.

As the end of the school day approached, I became more and more nervous, I had decided that I needed to try and avoid leaving school at the regular time as everyone else, so I had come up with a plan, if I played up in last class, and refused to do my work. I would be kept behind. I knew that I would have to explain to dad why I was late, but I guessed a slap off him was better than the gang of six girls, kicking the shit out of me. I had seen them fighting in the past, and they were nasty pieces of work. So, the last lesson I did precisely, what I had planned. I sat in my chair, making stupid noises and refused to do any of my work.

My teacher Mr. Bright was such a moody teacher anyway, so it was easy to wind him up, the more I pushed him, the louder he would shout at me. I had gotten used to being screamed at when I was at home, so it didn't bother me, but it bothered Mr. Bright, he started to go red with rage as he dragged me out of the classroom by my blazer. He ordered me to stand in the corridor, and he would come and get me at the end of the lesson. My plan had worked. I sat on the floor, feeling very proud of myself. The end of the school day had come, and I was waiting to be taken back to my class so Mr. Bright could make me do the work I had missed.

I walked into the classroom; I saw Julie stood by Mr. Bright's desk, she had been told another girl who was in my last lesson, that I had been kicked out of class and I was being kept behind after school to avoid the fight.

Julie had told Mr. Bright that she didn't understand the homework the other science teacher had set her.
She was making out that she needed him to explain it to her. Julie was asked to sit at the back of the classroom, and that he would look at the homework set for her after he had sorted my lesson plan for me, she walked past my chairs and whispered.

'Nice try baby, I will see you in a bit' and she went and sat down.

I could feel her starting at the back of my head; I was scared stiff, I didn't want any trouble, I would be in enough trouble when I got home, so the last thing I needed was a kicking from her as well. I finished my work and was told I could leave, Julie was still talking to Mr. Bright, so I had hoped I could run home before she got out.

I was wrong, as I got to the underpass at the bottom of the road, I seen the other five girls waiting for me. None of them were in their school uniforms, and I knew if they got changed first they were ready to fight, at least that way if a member of the public tried to get involved, they couldn't grass you up if they didn't know what school you attended. The kids of Manchester would usually have a set of clothes in their school bags called their fighting gear. They really did give me a good beating that day; my arms were red raw from protecting my face as they tried to stamp on my head.

A man walking his dog had seen what was happening and came to my, recuse. The kind man knelt beside me and told me not to move while he rang the police.
He said I need to go to the hospital to make sure I was okay. I didn't want any of that, and I just needed to get home.

I explained to him, as I tried to get myself off the ground. My stomach was really painful from my operation a few months before; I was a heap on the floor when the girls ran off away laughing and giggling to themselves, but I managed to walk home. It just took a lot longer than usual what with the pain I was feeling.

As I got to my front door, my mum was standing in the doorway waiting for me

'It's almost five o clock, where the hell have you been?' she asked, 'Your dad is out looking for you, where the hell have you been?'

I told her what had happened in class and how I got detention to avoid getting beat up and showed her my bruises from getting a kicking, she just shook her head and said,

'It sounds like it served you right; you should learn to fight them, shouldn't you?'

Dad had returned home about half hour after me, and mum must have told him what had, happened, he stormed up the stairs and barged into my bedroom, telling how fucking stupid I was, and then he lent down towards me and growled in my face.

'Are you trying to get yourself noticed?

I didn't know what exactly he meant by that comment, but I was angry, and I snapped back

'More like you're scared of me being noticed, dad!'
I could see in his face as he bubbled with rage that he was afraid of being caught, I thought I had one over him, but it was set just to make him even worst,

'You are a stupid little bitch who deserves a beating every now and again, ' and with that, he punched me full force on the side of my head.

I fell back into my bed, and he stood over me. He lent down towards me and whispered,

'Even easier to kick the fuck out of you when we can blame someone else for the bruises, just you remember that love' he hissed in my face, and half laughed as he turned and walked back out of my bedroom.

My dad really scared me that night, and I couldn't sleep very well, I just kept going over what he had said, but little did I realize, my one comment about him fearing me being noticed would lead to the scariest day of my life.

My Darkest Hour...

So, my week just got worst as the days went on, but it was coming up to the weekend, and I was allowed to go to my friend Sabrina's thirteenth birthday party on Saturday. Even more strangely, I was told I could stay over. Sabrina was a bit older than me, but we became friends very quickly, she was a very sporty type of girl and played for Manchester United junior girls team, she had done so since she was nine.

I was close to her, even though I wasn't sporty at all, we both loved the band Take That and the football team Manchester United. For about a year Sabrina was our next-door neighbor, so, my parents trusted me going to her house when they moved a few streets away from us. Apart from when I was at school, dad wouldn't let me out of his sight, so it was a relief to know I was away from school and home for a little while at least.
That Saturday mum had walked me to meet Sabrina by the shops on the corner of our street. I hadn't been to her house because her parents wanted to decorate before they had visitors around.

We only saw each other at school during break times, and in our English lesson with Mr. Wright, he was a grey-haired old teacher who liked to spend more time reading a book than teaching his class. We knew the lesson itself as the dossing class, so we would sit at the back of the class talking about how amazing Take-That were.

It was at the back of our English class when Sabrina had told me I had to make sure I could come to her party. She knew I liked a boy in our year called Aaron and she had invited him especially for me, so I was over the moon when my dad said I could go. Dad said it would be nice to get rid of me for the night, which sounded ironic considering he hated me out of his sight. As mum and I arrived at the shop where Sabrina was waiting for me, I said my goodbyes, but my mum asked me to kiss her on the cheek. Which really annoyed me, I was eleven, 'How embarrassing' I said to my mate once mum was out of earshot. We popped into the shop to get some things Sabrina had been asked to pick up, and we made our way towards her house.

'You should see my new computer' she said with a big smile on her face, I just smiled back at her 'can't wait' I muttered.
I was slightly jealous because her family had money as her parents had always worked hard and Sabrina was spoilt rotten because of it, not bitchy spoilt though. She just knew she could get anything she asked her dad. Being an only child, her parents could give her anything she wanted, and I really envied that, my parents never had money and I would be lucky if they brought me new things, most of the time everything I owned was either secondhand or my cousins hand me downs.

Her new house looked massive, compared to my run-down old council house. The pouch was the size of my bedroom, and I was amazed. We spent most of the afternoon in her bedroom listening to our favorite band and talking about boys. Tara had popped round to see us; she had bitched at me for not going to her house like planned the weekend before.

I told her I was grounded, but in all honesty, I hated going around her house because it just reminded me of being at home, her parents where pot smoking wannabe hippies, but, they lived like pigs. My house wasn't much better, but it was clean, I can say that much. Tara's dad was sleazy as well; I always felt his stare on me when we were sat in the same room, and it was the same sick shivering feeling I felt every time I sat in the same place as my father.

The weekend flew by, and the party was really good fun, I hadn't the courage to talk to Aaron, and within an hour he was kissing Chole, Sabrina's sister. I didn't mind though because in all honesty I wasn't even interested in boys that way. Sabrina, Tara and I all sat up that evening after everyone else had gone home and it must have been about four in the morning when we finally settled to sleep.

I slept like a baby and remembered thinking that it was soon time for me to go home. I didn't want to leave, but I knew that this wasn't the life I deserved.

I was waiting for my mum to turn up to walk me home, I had spoken to her on the phone the night before, and she said she would be at Sabrina's by 3 o'clock in the afternoon, it was sunny, so we were in the front garden. Sabrina was trying to show me how to kick a ball, but I wasn't very good at it. Most of the time kicking the air instead of the ball, but we were in fits of giggles. For some reason I looked behind me, and seen my dad standing across the road from us, looking at me, with that piercing stare,

'I best go' I said to Sabrina.

She gave me a concerned look as I picked my bag up off the floor.

'See you in school' she said and waved before going into her house.

As I walked up to my dad, I asked if he was okay.

'No, I'm fucking not' he answered and grabbed my arm to force me to start walking. We were walking in silence for about five minutes when he stopped walking and just stood there, he didn't say anything, and he just stared at me.

'What?' I asked.

'You know!' was his reply.

I didn't know what he meant, and then he asked what I had been laughing about. I told him it was because I couldn't play football, but he called me a liar, he said he knew what I had been doing, and he wouldn't let me get away with it, and then he started walking again. I caught up with him scared stiff of what he meant. He wasn't making any sense at all, and for the rest of the walk home he just kept repeating to himself,

'She will pay, she will pay.'

He didn't care if anyone heard him, it was like he was in a world of his own. We got to the road where we needed to cross over, but he carried on walking straight up the road towards town.

'Dad you're going the wrong way' I shouted, but he kept ignoring me, so I ran to catch up with him again.

'Where are we going?' I asked

'Home' he snapped.

I didn't want to argue, so I kept walking, my legs were getting tired, we were about ten-minute walk from home when we walked down a side street

'This way' dad snapped again 'and hurry the fuck up' he said.

I was struggling to keep up with him, and then he stopped outside a small red-bricked house, that I didn't recognize.

'Get in' he ordered, pointing to the door, so I placed my hand on the handle of the door a walked into the hallway.

Dad followed closely behind me and closed the door, he reached into his pocket and pulled out a set of keys and locked the front door.

'Your mothers in the kitchen' he said calmly pointing down the hall.

My mum was standing by the sink, unpacking our stuff out of old walker's crisps boxes.

'Have we moved to a new house again?' I asked confused.

'Didn't your dad tell you?' she replied with a concerned look on her face.

I had been away for thirty-one hours, and they had moved to a new house, our other house was a bit run down, but this new house didn't seem any better from my first impressions. I walked into the living room which was lead off the kitchen and seen some things in a box from my old bedroom,

'Can I take these upstairs?' I shouted through to the kitchen.

Mum didn't reply, but I heard dad shout me from upstairs. The living room was big, and it had a door on each side of the room, the door in front of me lead to the stairs so I picked up the box, which was heavier than I expected and started to walk. When I got to the top of the stairs, the twins were playing with toys in the one bedroom, and mum and dad's room was in the room next door, so I guess my room was at the bottom of the hall. When I got closer to my room, I saw my dad sat on a mattress on the floor.

'Where's my bed' I asked him as I placed the heavy box on the floor, but he didn't answer me he just walked out of my room and muttered

'I haven't forgotten.'

I thought he was acting a bit strange but took no real notice. I closed my door and started removing my things from the cardboard box and arranging them on the little wooden table by my mattress on the floor.

That evening, mum had made my bed for me, she apologized for not having a bed for me. She said dad had lost his temper on Saturday, while she was walking me to my friends and for some reason took it out on my bed. Mum said she would get me one soon, as she closed my curtains while I got undress in the bathroom.
When I got back to my room, she wasn't there.

Within seconds of me getting into bed, my parents were downstairs screaming and shouting at each other, they were so loud, that they woke Daniel up and he was crying hard.

I made the mistake of going downstairs to tell them that he was crying and had woke up Callum up as well. As soon as I got downstairs, I had wished I had just ignored the twins.

I walked into the living room and dad was standing over mum screaming in her face, he didn't notice me standing behind him, till mum asked me to go back to bed. I was about to walk out the room when my dad grabbed my hair and started pulling my head around, he was still screaming at mum, and he pulled my hair for me to face him, he stared straight into my eyes with that piercing, almost hollow look and scowled

'It's your fault, now she knows, and it's your fucking fault.'

Mum was screaming at him to let go of me, and he ignored her, as he tightened his grip around my hair I was punched in the side of my ribs so hard that I nearly lost my balance.

'That's for crying you little slag.'

He pulled me towards the kitchen, with one hand firmly wrapped around my hair, his other hand reached for the kitchen drawers. He was pulling all sorts out and slamming them on the worktop until he found what he was looking for.

The most prominent knife we had in the house, it was a seven-inch stainless steel blade with a Wilkinson Sword brand etched on to it and a greyish blue four-inch handle.

I was screaming at him begging to let me go, but he just pulled my hair tighter around his grip.

He was pulling my hair out when I heard my mum shouting to leave me alone, dad turned around and smiled at me before letting me go.

I fell to the floor screaming for help, mum had run into the kitchen, and he pushed past her dragging me across the floor by my hair. I was petrified, I thought he had stabbed my mum when he pushed past her, but she got up off the floor. Crying and begging on her knees for him to let me go.

'It wasn't my fault Laura' he said.

By this point, he was crying now, and he let go of my hair again. I soon as I felt him release his grip, I ran towards the other end of the room. Falling over my own feet as I shuffled myself behind the chair. I was sobbing my heart out, but no noise left my lips. I was sure he wanted to kill me. With my head buried in my knees and sobbing hard, I didn't hear or see Daniel coming down the stairs, he was rubbing his face, and his eyes were all red from all the crying himself. Mum and dad had stopped arguing; the room was quiet as dad called my little brother over to sit by him. I peeped my head around the chair; mum looked scared stiff.

'Please love, don't' she begged.

'Don't be stupid' dad responded with 'It will all be fine' and pointed for her to stay where she was on the chair.

I moved from the side of the chair and coward beside my mum's feet.

'You here' dad pointed to me then pointed to a space on the other side of him

'Mum?' I begged, hoping to God that she would tell me I didn't have to sit by him.

She just nodded at me and said, 'go on, it is okay now, we're all okay now.'

I sat beside my dad, my brother on the other side of him while mum was trying her best not to argue with him, but it was hard not to argue when she had just found out that dad was 'inappropriate with me' as he had put it. He told her it was only once, and she seemed to be forgiving him. I was angry, and I shouted at him.

'No, it wasn't, you are a liar'.

He looked at me and shook his head. Dad looked at Daniel who had somehow fallen back to sleep on the sofa. He then looked back at me and said.

'Why do you make me do these things Sarah, can't you see what you are doing' with that he grabbed my hair again and pulled my head close to his.

'Sorry to do this but you will never learn' he then pulled the knife up towards me and told me not to move, or the blade might cut straight through me.

Mum was begging him to let me go, whispering her plea as I sat beside him more scared than I ever thought were possible.

As I swallowed, the blade seemed to press against my neck even harder.
The fear and panic ran through my veins, and I could hear my heartbeat inside my ears. I closed my eyes as tears flooded my face, and I could feel the cold, sharp metal against my neck as I tried to swallow again.

I needed to swallow the saliva, which was building up in my mouth, but I thought if I swallowed too hard the blade would just rip through my skin.

I had seen enough messed up stuff on television to know a slice to the throat is game over, those few minutes felt like forever as I started to think of everything. It was like all my life was flashing through my mind at once, and I was sure this is what the end of my life was going to be like. Eventually, I learned to swallow slowly, making me have more control over the blade. Mum and dad had been talking while my mind was in overdrive, so even though I heard what they were saying I never really took in anything that was said. Dad's arm had loosened, so the blade was resting ever so slightly on my neck now.

Me swallowing apparently got his attention though as he gripped my hair tighter and placed the knife against my throat again, resting it just under my chin. I felt the blade push harder against me and I was sure it had cut through my skin, the next thing I knew I could feel a warm wet feeling under my bum. I was so scared that I had wet myself and it didn't take long for my dad to notice as well. He moved the seven-inch blade away from my neck and pushed me to the floor. My hand went up to my throat, but luckily it was just a scratch, and the blade hadn't pierced my skin.

'You, dirty little bitch, get washed and get to fucking bed.'

I scrambled off the floor as fast as I could and ran up the stairs, banging my shin of the second from the top step and almost falling head first into the bathroom door. I closed the door and locked it behind me.

I was shaking like crazy and sobbing uncontrollably.

After I had calmed down I stood myself up a walked towards the mirror over the sink, I could see where the blade had been pushed into my skin on my neck, and I was now scared stiff to leave the bathroom, never mind go to bed.

So, I just lay on the bathroom floor and sobbed myself to sleep on a dirty, damp towel. I didn't ever want to wake up, I hated myself for being alive, I hated the fact that I was so openly hated by my dad, and I never knew why. The next morning, I had woken still on the bathroom floor, I could hear movement on the other side of the bathroom as I stumbled onto my knees and growled to myself as my whole body ached. I pulled myself up using the edge of the sink and stood to stare at myself in the mirror. My neck was still red, and tears started to fill my eyes,

'How could my dad want to kill me' I thought to myself.

I just stood staring at my now distorted reflection from my teary eyes; I was holding onto the sink that hard, that my palms of my hands were really starting to hurt. Shaking with fear, anger, and frustration. At that point, I had decided that I couldn't carry on living like this and planned in my head, how I just wouldn't return home from school.

I had decided that I wouldn't be missed anyway so that everyone would be happy. My thought process was interrupted by a big bang on the bathroom door.

'Hurry up in there, for fuck sake' my dad bellowed.

I turned to look at the door and make sure it was still locked and set back to look at my reflection,
'Sarah Louise, Open the fucking door, your brother needs a piss.'

Nervously, I opened the door and walked into my bedroom, closing the door behind me. I sat on my mattress on the floor, my head on my knees and my arms wrapped around the front of them. I held myself so tightly. I didn't want my dad to see me crying because he seemed to get off on upsetting me and I didn't want to give him that satisfaction. My door opened, but it was my mother; she said I needed to get ready for school. I just looked up at her as if to say 'really' she looked back at me and said,

'You can go to school, or you can stay with him' she was referring to my dad.

'No, it's okay, I will go to school.'

I got my things ready to get dressed. My body still hurt from sleeping on a cold, damp floor all night, and I hoped my mum would have said something about me sleeping on the floor, but I should have known better than to think she cared. It didn't get mentioned all morning. I was ready to walk out of the door to make my way to school, I wasn't a hundred percent sure which way I had to walk since we had just moved the day before, but I didn't care I just wanted to get out of the house. I had told myself that I would know which way to go once I got out of our street so, I grabbed my coat off the pile of coats that were thrown in a heap at the bottom of the stairs. I was just about ready to leave, when my dad called me into the living room, I was scared but knew I had to do what he said, so walked sheepishly through the living room door with my head looking down at my shoes. He was stood the other side of the door.

'Your mother wants you' he snapped pointing to the kitchen.

Mum was making a coffee and seen me walk in behind her

'Ready for school?' she asked all cheerful.

'Yep, can I go now?'

She said it was okay, but I needed to know that my dad was very sorry; she said that he gets stressed sometimes, but he still loved me.

'Yeah, sure he does' I muttered, so I turned to walk back to the living room, my dad was at the front door, holding it open for me.

'I will walk you' he said.

'It is okay' I assured him 'Sabrina is meeting me.'

'Well, you better keep your mouth shut! Do you fucking understand?' he snapped.

I nodded my head and walked out of the door. Sabrina wasn't really meeting me, but I just needed a reason to get out of the house, without him.

As I walked to the bottom of the road I seen a few other kids walking in a group just in front of me, they were older kids, probably in year ten or eleven but they had the same uniform as me, so I decided to follow them. I had been crying silently, with tears falling down my face. It didn't help that the wind was cold and sharp on my wet cheeks and my nose was running like mad so, by the time I arrived at school I went straight to the girl's toilets.

I really needed to sort myself out, the last thing I needed was to be asked what was wrong with me because I was scared I would tell all, and the aftermath would be too much to handle.

Once I had calmed down and washed the tears from my face, I went to my tutor's classroom and stood outside waiting, I was the first one to line up, which wasn't like me at all.

I was usually late for most of my lessons, so when my teacher walked up to our classroom to unlock our door,

'You are an early bird Sarah' she said with a gentle voice.

I gave her a half smile and walked into the classroom behind her, I sat on my chair and got my planner out ready to be told what classrooms our lessons would be in that day. All the classes were numbered, each with a letter from them, to make it easier for us to find our classrooms with little or no problems. The classroom started to fill up, the sound of everyone chatting at once was hurting my head, so I placed my head on the table and looked down at my feet.

'Penny for them' someone said as they sat beside me, it was June.

She sat beside me and asked what was wrong with me. I told her I was fine, she left it at that, but I could see her concern in her eyes.

'I'm always here to talk to' she said.

I just nodded back with a crooked smile and told her I was fine, and she needn't worry about me. I sat up straight in my chair and rearranged my blazer.

'Oh my god' she gasped. I didn't know what she was on about and just looked at her confused

'Your neck' she said, she had said it so loud that out teacher had walked over to the table we were sat at.

'Let me have a look' my teacher asks as she leaned down towards me.

'It's nothing' I said, worried sick she would know what had happened.

'It was my brother messing about miss, honestly.'

I must have sounded like I was lying because she acted like she didn't believe me. By this point, the whole classroom had gone quiet, and I could feel everyone staring at me 'I'm fine' I snapped.

I pushed my table away from me; I grabbed my bag and ran out of the classroom. I ran so hard up the corridor, one of the teachers was shouting me to stop running, but I just ignored them and ran into the girl's toilets. I locked myself in the bathroom cubical and sat on the toilet with my feet up and my knees on my chest, I hugged myself so tight, rocking backward and forward on the seat of the toilet.

I was shaking so hard that I almost lost my balance and walked my shoulder on the wall of the cubical. That pissed me off even more, and I hated everything about my life, my parents, my school, my home, but most of all I hated myself. If it was just my dad who seemed to hate me then I think I could have coped better, but with my school life getting worst and bullying appeared to be a game to some of the pupils in my year. I had convinced myself, that it was my fault that everyone hated me, and I honestly believed everyone would be happier if I just got it over and done with.

I thought it would be easier to kill myself rather than live this life. My dad would probably kill me off soon enough anyway, so I decided to save him the trouble. I didn't know how I would do it, but I had convinced myself it was the only thing I could do. Sad really, I was only an eleven-year-old girl, just eleven years on this planet and I wanted out already.

Getting a Grip on Life…

So, the abuse carried on as usual. Each weekend when mum was at work, dad would come in my room and make me suck him off. He started to do more things to me, and he knew I hated it. I was told to get used to it, he said that that's what I was here for and reminded me that it was my mother's fault. He said if I needed to blame someone, to blame her. Dad must have got used to me doing my mum's job because it seemed to last even longer. Before when it first started to abuse me, I knew that the quicker I did what he told me, the better it was for me.

Now the abuse was going on for just over an hour at a time. He said he needed to have a break in between and would send, me to the bathroom to wash before my dad would 'please me again' as he called it.
There is nothing pleasing about his panting red face being between my legs, I even started to push him away, but he would just punch me in the stomach and force me to lie down, I knew it was easier to just cope with it. I had to ignore the blood boiling inside my veins.

I could feel every pump of my weak heart and could feel it even more so when my heart forgot to beat every now and again.
I knew I had to try and take my mind off what he was doing to me and what he was making me do to him, so I start thinking of ways out, thinking of a way I could end all this bullshit I called my life. I had decided enough was enough.

It had been a few weeks since my outburst at school, and the teachers had started to talk about me in the staffroom. I have overheard my tutor asking my science teacher to keep an eye on me. God knows what had I done wrong I thought to myself. I hated all the attention and started to skip school; I would end up at the shopping Centre, walking around the town, window shopping of course because I never had any money. I could feel the shopkeepers looking at me; I hated the fact that they all thought that if you were young and not in school, it meant you were on the rob, which had offended me because I had never stolen in my life. I decided to walk out of town, but I had never been out of the town center on my own and got myself a little lost. I was away from home and school, so I didn't panic if anything I felt calm. I was walking along the main road, and I could see the steeple off the old church in the background, so decided that was where I was heading.

While we lived in Ireland, it had been drummed into me that I was a good Catholic girl and should go to church every week. I didn't mind doing it, in fact, I enjoyed the peace and security that came with being in the holy place of worship, I felt safe, which was a rare feeling. Since we had moved to Manchester though, I never got to go to church, mum couldn't be bothered, and dad said it was bullshit he only put up with in front of his mother, my father's mum was a small, religious Irish lady, strict but also very fair and kind natured. So as soon as I see the steeple, I knew where I had to be.

As I got to the chapel, it was massive. An oversized building, much bigger than the churches I had seen and been to in Ireland.
The dark stone brick seemed to go up higher than I could even see.

I imagined it was a stairway towards heaven. I did have a fantastic imagination at the sweet age of eleven. The sun reflected on the stained-glass windows, and the vast archway doors were open, so I walked towards them. The church was an array of colors as the sun shone through the windows. Like a magical kaleidoscope. The mosaic tiled floor was a river of bright sun rays; I stood there in complete ore of the building. I almost jumped because I hadn't noticed the vicar walking towards me.

'Welcome child' he said and placed his hand out to beckon me inside the building

I walked towards him, and he asked if I want to take a seat. I was uneasy and felt nervous being on my own with him, but he seemed friendly enough as I sat beside him on the church pew which looked like the benches we used to get in primary school. He asked me why I wasn't at school and I started to explain that life sucks and I didn't know what to do. I went on to explain about life at home, without letting him know of the sexual abuse I had encountered. The vicar looked worried and asked if I wanted to talk to someone who could help, but I refused his concerns and said I would be okay

'God only hands out thought times the strongest of people, God must think you are a strong one' he said reassuringly patting me on the head as he got up. 'I will leave to think about it' he said as he got up and walked back towards the altar.

I looked down at my watch and realized I needed to get back on the bus to return home otherwise my parents would know I hadn't gone to school, so I left the chapel and made my way back to the bus station at the Trafford Centre.

I was sure my parents wouldn't notice if I got home in time anyway, but I wasn't willing to take the chance.

As the bus pulled up to the station, I saw my mother stood at the bus stop waiting. I panicked and ducked behind my seat, I had hoped she didn't get on the bus and let it drive on but the bus stopped, and I was sure I was to be caught out. She didn't get on, and the bus carried on past her, we got to the next stop, and I got off.
I was scared, why else would mum be waiting if it weren't because she knew I would be on the bus I also wondered where dad and the twins were. It was almost three thirty, and I was due to home any minute. As I walked around the corner, I saw mum walking into our house, so I followed behind her and acted as nothing had happened.

'Did you have a good day?' she asked as I walked through the front door.

'Not bad' I said taking my schoolbag off my back,

'What did you learn?' she asked.

'Not much.'

I had a feeling she knew I hadn't been to school but just answered her questions a vague as I could, so I wasn't exactly lying to her. My dad was out which was usual, he had gone to his mates to play cards and mum had said I best get to my bedroom before he got home. I walked upstairs and got my English book out. I wanted it to look like I had homework to do, but of course, I had no homework because I hadn't been to school. Mum walked upstairs about half hour later, she sat on my mattress and said,

'By the way, I wasn't born yesterday.'

I must have looked guilty as she looked me in the eyes.

'Sorry' I said, and she got up to walk back out of my room.

Dad had returned a few hours later, the twins and I had eaten our dinner, and we were upstairs getting ready for bed, mum must have told him I had skipped school, he stormed into my room, demanding to know where I had been. I lied and told him I had been in school, the rage in his face soon was back and he started hitting me repeatedly over the head,

'You stupid, fucking, bitch' he was repeating the words over and over again while swinging his fist into the back of my head, harder and harder.

'Are you trying to get noticed' he shouted.

Hitting me on my shoulders and anywhere else he could reach, every time he missed, dad would get even angrier and punch me harder, and he missed a few times. I was screaming, he was shouting, and there was loads of banging, but mum stayed downstairs and ignored her tiny daughter getting beaten by a fully-grown man.

I should have known what to expect by now, but I still hoped that my mother would come to my rescue, even with all the abuse, I just wanted what every other child my age wanted, to feel loved and safe. Was I asking for too much? I realized things needed to change, and the sooner, the better.

That evening when everyone in the house was asleep, I crept down the stairs and walked into the kitchen.

I had decided a knife would be the most natural thing to use and had decided if I didn't think about it too much, it might not hurt for long, and it was worth it to get out of this hell hole I called my life.

I opened the kitchen drawer as quietly as I could, but as I opened the drawer. I started to feel sick, and I froze, stood there so still.

Maybe it was the realization of what I had planned to do, or perhaps it was because as I opened the drawer, I saw the big Wilkinson Sword knife dad had held to my throat weeks before, the same big knife he had been taking to bed to threaten my mother with every night.

Either way, the more I thought about it, the more the fear bubbled inside me, I couldn't stab myself, and I knew that I couldn't even try. I thought about stabbing my dad while he was asleep, but I feared what he would do if he caught me and that was enough for me to close the draw slowly and walk away.

I sat on the sofa; it must have been about two in the morning, I curled in a ball and couldn't believe how weak I was. I couldn't stand up to my dad, but I had the change to end everything, and I chickened out. Maybe I was meant to be a victim, perhaps that's the life God had chosen for me.

So, I thought about other things I could do, I lay there cold and sleepy and remembered June talking about her neighbor who tried to kill herself with tablets, so I had an idea.

I walked back into the kitchen and quietly pulled the chair up to the side. We had a medicine cupboard, but I was too small to reach it.

I was only just under four-foot-tall, the smallest in my year, which being in year seven made me the tiniest pupil at my school.

The back of the chair banged against the cupboard door as I clambered up, I froze for a second, making sure no one heard me when all I could hear my heartbeat in my head. I reached for the medicine cupboard; there were three packs of tablets. I wasn't sure what aspirin was at the time but knew that the pills in the red box were for pain relief, because I had seen my mum take them when she had a headache, and the emotional pain I was in made me sure that these would help.

I grabbed the blister of tablets from the box and climbed down as slowly as I could, trying not to disturb anyone in the house. I placed the chair back at the table and grabbed a glass off the drainer to pour myself some water; I had seen mum take tablets all the time, so guessed it would be easy. As I made my way back into the darkened living room and sat back down on my chair, I removed the tablets from the packaging, and place my water on the floor.

As each tablet popped out, I had a sense that it was all coming to an end. I was scared, but I couldn't do this anymore and placed four tablets in my mouth at once.

I grabbed my water and tried to swallow them, but it was no use.

I was choking and spilling more water over me than in my mouth, so I removed the tablets from my mouth, all wet and sticky in my fingers and tried with one at the time.

It was still no good, my body was stopping me from swallowing them, no matter how much I tried it made no difference, so I gave up. I placed the un-slobbered tablets back in the box and left them on the kitchen side. I was too sleepy to move the chair again, so I turned the kitchen light off and walked back up the stairs and climbed back into bed. I felt useless. I couldn't even take control of my own life when I had the chance.

'God must like to punish me' I muttered as I pulled my covers up to my neck.

The next morning, mum had noticed the tablets on the side and asked who had been messing about with them, I had told her I had a headache and tried to take one, but I couldn't swallow it,

'It's a good job you didn't' she said concerning. 'They are far too strong for you; one tablet would knock you out,' she said putting them back away.

'That's what I had been hoping' I muttered to myself, but she didn't hear me.

A Bumpy Road Ahead...

During the summer holidays, I had celebrated my twelfth birthday; I didn't have a party or any mates to invite, it was just the twins, mum, and dad and me. My parent brought me a Take-That bed cover, and a new bed to replace the old smelly mattress on the floor that I had had since coming out of the hospital. Mum told me she had a surprise for me; I was excited, maybe they had brought me the new hair studio accessories kit I had asked for at Christmas.

I waited, and mum pulled out a pregnancy test, she told me she was pregnant again and that it was a fresh start for all of us. How the hell, was mum having a baby going to help me in any way, I thought to myself. Apart from mum maybe being at home more often, I couldn't see any benefit at all, dad would still beat me in front of her, so I didn't understand what she meant by a fresh start. I didn't care anymore anyway. Mum went on the explain that we were moving again.

'Where to this time' I asked with a cocky grin on my face,

'Back to your Nan's' she replied.

I lit it up like a bloody Christmas tree; In my head, I would be safe in Crosby with my nan. I hadn't seen her in years but remembered how sweet she was to me. So, I had finally seen some peace at the end of all this shit.

Within a week we were back in Crosby, living at nans while mum found us a house.

It wasn't the same as I remembered, and I don't mean the décor of the house, it didn't feel the same.

Nan was less argumentative with my mum and dad but didn't bother with me and the twins anymore, my mum's younger sister Margo had a little boy called David, and my nan doted on him. They shared the close relationship, I use to have with my nan. It didn't bother me, it was nice to see the closeness they had, and it just made me realize that I didn't have that type of love in my life.

I had started a new school; the twins were at home as mum found it harder to get them back into education, I was in year one still of secondary school, we left Manchester, halfway through my term.
It was hard to make friends at the best of times, and I had a strong mixed accent still from living in Belfast and then back to England. The kids at school always had this stigma with anyone new, the boys in my class would call me names and the girls would get me to repeat everything and then giggle to themselves.

I didn't think I sounded any different, but those kids really did. I met one girl called Annabelle, she was a lot taller than me with long blonde hair, she was nice and took me under her wing. We hung around with each other every break time, and if I were allowed that week, I would go to Anna's for dinner on the Friday after school. Most of her family were nice. Anna's mum was always friendly towards me; she was a single mum to five kids. Anna had two older brothers.

One of which I never met because he was in prison for grievous bodily harm. Anna's other brother Tony was a few years older than us; he made me feel uneasy, from the first day I met him he acted weird in front of me, whispering that I was beautiful and had lovely eyes.

I didn't like him one bit, and Anna knew I didn't, so most of our time was spent in her bedroom with her sister Kellie, she had a different dad to the other kids. You could tell because she had a Spanish look to her, and naturally beautiful. She was older and very confident. I think it annoyed her when Anna and I would talk about boys all giggly because Kellie was almost twenty and had a long-term boyfriend, so we must have seemed like little kids to her. Anna's younger sister Maggie was lovely; her real name was Margret, but she hated her old-fashioned name. Maggie used to let me and Anna dress her up and put makeup on her, she felt like a princess.

I loved going to Anna's house, and even though her brother was a creep, it was worth it just to get some normality in my life.
One afternoon when we were messing about upstairs, Anna and Maggie has found some vodka and thought it would be a clever idea to get drunk.

So, we passed the bottle around and each took a swig. It was burning my mouth, and it reminded me of that horrible new year's party. I tried to forget it, and we carried on drinking a mouthful, complaining how awful it was and passing the bottle on. I was starting to feel tipsy, and we were all giggly, but for some reason, I couldn't get the abuse at home out of my head, I tried to plaster a fake smile on my face and carried on doing stupid voices and pulling faces trying to make each other laugh.

We were in the back garden and I drunkenly started kissing a big water fountain; it was shaped like a mermaid, Anna was in stitches laughing at me and commented on me being a lesbian when I was older.

'Wouldn't surprise me with a dad like mine' I replied

'What do you mean?' Maggie asked, we sat on the grass, and I told Anna and Maggie all about my life at home.

Anna told me she had guessed, and she said her uncle was abusive to her and that's why they left Liverpool. Her dad hadn't believed her, but her mum didn't want to take any chances, so the moved to Crosby to get away. She went on to say that she could see it in my eyes and that scared me because if Anna could see it then who else could?

When I got home mum and dad had found a house just around the corner from my nans which is ideal for mine and the twin's new schools.

We seemed a lot more settled, the abuse still happened but not as often, and dad seemed a little less stressed all the time. My parents were waiting on the birth of their new baby and that summer holidays mum had given birth to my baby brother, he was so tiny with soft, gentle skin. I was so proud to be a big sister again.

They named him Matthew; I had used my pocket money to buy my new baby brother a tiny teddy to put in his Moses basket. I had spent weeks saving, and I was so excited when mum arrived home from the hospital.

Matthew looked perfect wearing his baby grow and blue knitted cardigan. As mum placed him in his new bed, I ran upstairs to fetch the teddy I had for him. I walked back in the living room, and I heard my dad telling my mum that they had no reason to stay anymore, I didn't know what they were talking about, but I knew better not to ask. I walked up to Matthew's crib and placed the teddy beside him. My dad was the closest to me and he reached into the Moses basket and removed the teddy.

'He can't have that in there, he's too fucking young' he snapped.

'Why didn't you say when we bought it?' I asked, but I just got told to go upstairs and stop answering back.

I sat in my room and wrote in the diary I had owned since my birthday. I found every evening I would write a few words before I went to bed. I was so angry I had to write it down there and then and as I wrote the words down my hands started shaking. I was trying my hardest to stop myself crying I hate my dad so much; he makes my life a living hell. I slammed the book closed, and I put it back under my mattress, I then lay down on my bed and closed my eyes and must have dozed off to sleep for a few hours.

A few months past and nothing changed, as normal dad still abused me anytime he had the chance too, and it had got to the point that I was used to it, and I had even started to accept that this was how things were meant to be.

It was the start of December, by this point I was twelve, and I had returned home from school one day to find my mum sat by the telephone crying her heart out, she was perched on the wooden chair with her knees up to her chest holding tightly onto the phone. I gently removed the receiver and placed it back on the phone and asked her what was wrong.

'Your dad has left' she sobbed.

I didn't know what to say, so I didn't say anything, then she looked at me with her tear-filled eyes and said.

'I bet you're happy now.'

I didn't know what to think but seeing my mother so upset, sure as hell, didn't make me happy.

I think the best way to describe what I felt was a relief. A few weeks passed, and mum was crying most of the time, she must have loved that monster, but I could never understand why.

On the Move Again...

I woke up to the sound of banging from my brother's bedroom, it was early in the morning and still dark outside. The first week in January and school had broken up for the Christmas holidays, but for me, Christmas came and went like an average day. Before the holiday's; everyone in my class seemed excited about their time off school. Everyone except me. That morning as I climbed out of bed and stood my door. I heard more banging and scuffling; the twins room was next to mine, so you could hear everything through the walls. I was expecting to see the twins playing but instead as I walked into their room I saw my mum packing all the toys away, in the same boxes she had unpacked just a few months before.

'What are you doing?' I asked.

'We are moving back to Ireland' she said calmly.

'When?'

'Today, Sarah, today' she sighed.
She sent me in my room with a box and told me to start packing, so I did. Later, in the day we got into a big blue and tan colored coach, with just a few bags of clothes. We sat down at the back, me, mum Matthew and the twins and made our way to Belfast port. It was late in the afternoon, and I had slept most of the journey.
When we arrived at the dock a whole three hours later, we climbed off the large bus, grabbed our bags and made our way towards to boat.

The boat was white with a big black line, running through the middle, it was massive, so high I couldn't see where the top of the ship ended.

I was not looking forward to moving yet again, but never really had a choice. The trip on the boat was so dull, and mum didn't have much money, so we didn't go to the arcades or cinema on the boat like I did when we traveled in the past, mum was quiet and left me to look after the kids. So, I spent most of the time in the soft play area keeping the twins amused.

Once we arrived in Belfast we made our way to my Granny's house and to be honest I wasn't looking forward to seeing my dad again, but I was excited at seeing my Granny and Auntie Amy. We were sat in the taxi and mum started to explain that dad was in a hospital for people who were sick in the head,

'Like a Looney bin?' I asked giggling to myself.

'It's not funny Sarah, you dads not well.'
He has never been well in the head I quietly thought to myself. I was relieved when we got to my Granny's house because the estate didn't look any different, it was like walking back in time, but just me being a few inches taller.

My gran was waiting outside in the garden. She was a small old lady, slightly curvy with curly grey hair and glasses. She put her arms out to me as the taxi door opened and I ran into her embrace, her blue, soft cardigan rubbed softly on my face, and she told me how much she had missed all of us.
She beckoned us into the house as it was cold in Northern Ireland, in fact, it was cold most of the time over there and from what I usually remember, very windy.

We all settled in that night and mum told me I would be starting school the next day. She explained that auntie Amy had sorted the school out for me a few weeks beforehand; I was slightly annoyed with my mum because she had known for weeks that we were moving back to Ireland, but didn't think to tell me till the day we were leaving.

I had asked about my uniform and she said to me that Amy friend's daughter had a spare uniform for me, 'Great' I thought to myself.
Not only was I rushed into starting a new school where I didn't know anyone, but I would have to wear someone else uniform.

I wasn't happy at all. Amy had the idea that if I met her friend's daughter, Stacey, that I would be able to try on the uniform, so we knew it fit me. Amy walked me across the road to meet them. Amy knocked on the door, and we waited for someone to answer the door.

'You will like Stacey' she said very matter of a fact.
'She is the same age as you, but I little taller, that why I guessed her uniform would fit you.'

Just then the door open and a small girl not much taller than me looked me up and down, then put her head back in the door and shouted

'Mammy Amy Brown and some other girls at the door' she then looked at me again with a slight smirk and said, 'You best come in then.'

She opened the door wider and ushered us inside, so we didn't let the dogs out.

When we got inside Stacey and I were sent upstairs to try old uniform on, I was waiting in her bedroom for a few minutes when she returned with a big pile of clothes she placed them on her bed and told me to try them on,

'What here?' I asked shocked.

'Yes, silly we are both girls.' So, I started to undress leaving my underwear on, she noticed the bruises and scars all over my legs, luckily for me, my scar from my operation was covered with my underwear.

'Wow, what happened to you' she asked concern.
I made up some story about play fighting with my brothers all the time, and she seemed to believe me.

'you will be best with trousers' she said looking at the big scars on my back of my legs.

I felt uncomfortable and the need to explain

'that one is my birthmark'

I went on to explain that when I was born, I had a strawberry birthmark which got infected when I was a few weeks old. It was the truth, but she looked at me like I was telling fibs. After I had finished putting on my uniform, I went downstairs with Stacey to show the adults.

Amy said the uniform fit me perfect and to be fair, it all looked new enough. As we were getting ready to go back to my Granny's, Stacey had asked me if I wanted to meet her the next morning, to walk to school.
She had said I would be in her year and mentioned that if we weren't in the same class that she would meet me at break time anyway, it was lovely knowing I had made a friend before I had even started a school.

Not bad for one day I thought to myself laying in my granny's living room that night. Matthew and mum were in Granny's spare room, and she has said she would sort the other room for me the next day.

I didn't mind sleeping on the sofa, and I had my Gran's little Chichewa dog to keep me company. She was a skinny tan colored dog and smaller than your average puppy, it was the fact that she was so small that I took a shine to her. I had always been small for my age, and usually, I was the smallest in my year.
I had wondered if it would be the case again.
I lay there that night trying my hardest to fall asleep, but I had a strange feeling that I wasn't used to and it made me overthink.
Then it dawned on me, I felt safe, and looking forward to the next day, and looking forward to seeing my new friend Stacey again.

The next morning, I was so excited and was washed and dressed by seven o clock, which wasn't like me at all. I was always the one to get shouted at in the morning because I took too long to get ready. I sat down at the kitchen table which my gran had set out all nicely with toast and jams, she had made me porridge and said I needed a filling breakfast for my first day at school. In my opinion, my Granny made the best food; it didn't matter what she cooked it always turned out perfect.

Just after eight Stacey knocked the door for me, I grabbed my empty schoolbag and coat, kissed my Granny on the head and walked out the front door.

My mum and brothers were all still asleep, so I closed the door quietly behind me.

My Life in His Hands

The walk to school was a completely straight line down the road for about ten minutes, my new school was Catholic, and the school next door was Protestant which was brave considering we were in Northern Ireland.
On the way to school, Stacey was telling me all about my new school, who the most helpful teachers were, who were considered the fittest boys and which girls to stay away from because they were known as troublemakers or bullies.

As we got to the school gates, I started to feel nervous; all the excitement had faded as soon as I seen the pupils outside, it seemed a lot bigger than Saint Paul's in Manchester.

What happens if no one likes me? I was an English girl. Starting an Irish Catholic school, inevitably, they would all hate me. I think Stacey could tell I was nervous, but she reassured it would all be okay and then walked with me to the reception where I had to meet a teacher who would show me around the school before taking me to my first lesson.

I walked up the corridor, I seen a young teacher with short shoulder length dark hair and glasses, she looked friendly enough, she was waiting for me, so I said my goodbyes to my new friend and walked over to the office door where the teacher was expecting me. I was asked to sign a few forms. She seemed surprised that my mum wasn't with me on my first day but said I could sign the paperwork anyway so wasn't a problem.

After the tour of the school, I was shown to the sports hall, my first lesson was P.E, but I was lucky because the lesson was almost over, so the teacher sent to over to the bench to sit and watch.

A ginger girl has sat down already so I sat next to her, she asked me loads of question and kept smiling when I spoke, I felt so uncomfortable then the P.E teacher called over to her.

'I thought you were sick, missus?'

'I am Miss the ginger girl replied, so we sat in silence for the rest of the lesson.

Once all the girls had been sent to get showered and changed the P.E teacher came over to see me, she asked what sports I liked, I wanted to say none, but didn't want to be cheeky so I told her I didn't know. She said I had to have an answer for Friday's lesson.

It was break time, and Stacey had told me to meet her on the steps by the All-Weather pitch. I didn't think to ask anyone, so I spent the first five minutes walking around. It was only after walking the whole way around the school that I noticed I had walked past the place I was to meet my new friend, and it was a big pitch not easy to miss really, but I was lost in a world of my own. I finally met up with Stacey and her friends, all the girls seemed nice enough, but I was getting sick of the consent questions everyone was asking, it was starting to do my head in, but I bit my tongue and smiled. By the end of the day, I was worn out. I hadn't taken much in the entire day, I just was bombarded with questions and couldn't wait to get home.

I stood outside the main school gates were Stacey said she was meeting me, it was cold, and I was tired and just wanted to walk home.

It was a straight line, so I wasn't going to get lost or anything, but I waited for her.

After twenty minutes, it was clear that she wasn't coming so I walked home on my own. I was annoyed that she had said she would meet me but then didn't, so I walked home in a huff, feeling sorry for myself.

I returned home, and my family was all asking me loads of different questions mainly about my first day at school. I made out my day was brilliant, so they would leave me alone, and it seemed to work.

As the month went on I had started to feel more at ease and had even begun to hang around with a group of girls; I had been bullied at all the other school I went to and decided that I wouldn't let it happen again. I had no control over it of course, but I decided that if I kept my head down all would be okay, and this worked for a while.

Even life at home seemed perfect, and with my dad still in Holywell hospital, I was safe. I knew at some point, he would be home because they wouldn't keep in a hospital for too long, and I was right.

Returning home from school on a lovely sunny afternoon in May. I was feeling nervous about going home for some reason but didn't know why; I had a gut feeling that something terrible had happened but couldn't figure out what it was. My mind was doing overtime with the endless possibilities of 'what if's' and I would be home soon enough, so I gathered pace and walked home with my head down.

As I walked into my Granny's back garden I could see the back door was open, when I walked into the kitchen I heard my dad's voice from the living room next door, and slowly walked towards the room, and there he was.

I felt sick, but I knew I had to show my face. He looked skinnier, and unclean with is new facial hair, he didn't even look at me once while I stood in the doorway, so, I made my way over to the empty chair in the other corner of the room.

We had spoken a few words, just hello and how are you, it was awkward, so I went into the kitchen to do my homework. I could hear them all chatting as if nothing had happened and it annoyed me. I had overheard to my relief, that my dad was only on a day visit so, I stayed in the kitchen the whole time, and no one questioned me which made me wonder if maybe my they knew my secret too.

An hour or so later I heard my dad getting ready to leave, my legs started shaking under the table, and my heart was pumping hard.

I felt him walk towards the kitchen door and I automatically looked up at him. He said goodbye to me, for some reason he stared into my eyes.
I felt his stare burning into my pupils, and my eyes started to fill with tears. I stood up from the kitchen table and walked away, the last thing I wanted that man to see was me feeling weak.

I didn't see my dad for another few weeks; it was almost the summer holidays.

The next time I would see him was on my birthday, we had gone to the hospital to visit him. The visit wasn't too bad, and all I remember was sitting outside on a bench.

It wasn't that warm considering it was the middle of June, dad was playing football with the boys, Mum was inside talking to a man dressed in a white doctor's coat.

We had been there for half an hour and ended up leaving a few minutes after my mum returned, back outside to join us.

Something in the Wind...

It was about two weeks into my nine-week summer holidays when my dad finally returned home, by then mum had got us a new house just a few doors from my Granny's and Amy's houses, so we were all living very close to each other.

In some ways, this gave me the protection I needed.

The day my father returned home I was out at my friend's house Claire's. She was taller than me but younger with long dark hair. Claire didn't have many friends really because she got teased a lot from the other kids our age, she had a scar on her top lip which trailed up to her nose from numerous operations when she was younger. Her looks should never have been a problem, and I felt for her because she was so loving and kind, but most of the girls who lived in Ballymore were just plain nasty.

Claire and I hit it off straight away, and I spent most of the summer with her. We had been writing our own songs when there was a knock on her front door, Claire's younger brother answered and ran up the stairs to tell me Daniel was at the door and had said my mum wanted me, so I said my goodbyes and arranged to meet again after my dinner.

When I got home my dad was sat at the kitchen table, he looked older and frail and was banging on about God being his hero. I walked straight past him towards my mum who was peeling potatoes in the kitchen sink.

'Is dinner nearly ready?' I asked

'No, why don't you say hello to your dad?' she said.

I knew I best do what she asked, so I went over to the kitchen table and said hello to him.

'Oh, you're my friend now.'

I nodded my head not wanting to talk.
We sat in silence, both of us looking out of the patio doors where the boys were playing. I could hear mum muttering something but didn't hear what she said, then she turns to me and my dad and snapped

'Are you two, gonna hurry up and kiss and make friends, please? I can't cope with the stress.'

Kiss and make up, if only she knew what she had just said. All these little words went around my head the whole time I was sat at the table.
I was wondering if she knew what was happening when she was at work, and maybe she did know but wanted to ignore it. Either way, her use of words cut me deep, and I could see by my dad's face he knew I felt uncomfortable sat there with him.

'Go to your room if your just gonna sit with a face like thunder' dad snapped,

So, I gladly got up to walk out of the room.
I pushed my chair back under the table and started walking towards the door at the top of the kitchen which led to the stairs.

'What the hell is wrong with you today' mum asked as I walked past her, I shrugged my shoulders and walked into the hall.

I was stood at the bottom of the stairs, and I could hear mum talking, she was saying that I was always moody lately and that dad was best to ignore me, sounded good to me I thought as I walked up the stairs. I got to my bedroom and noticed the twins had been messing with the few things I owned, it annoyed me, and I ran down the stairs full of anger. I walked straight past my mum and dad in the kitchen towards the back door where it boys were playing

'Stay out of my room, for God's sake.'

I should have realized with dad's bible bashing, that was the wrong thing to shout out, but I was angry and honestly didn't care at that point. I didn't have much and didn't appreciate my brothers ruining everything.

'What did you just say?' I heard my dad ask, by this point he was stood behind me 'What the fuck did you just say to the twins?' he shouted.

'I told them to stay out of my room, that's all.'

'Fuck off now, you little bitch, how dare you' he continued 'you have no right, you don't have a room until you pay the rent, it's my fucking room.'

'The government pay your rent' angrily I bit back.

'Your cheeky bitch, who do you think you're talking too?'

He grabbed hold of my hair and dragged me into the living room, I was screaming for him to let go and he tossed me on the floor like a rag doll, he was still shouting at me calling me a cheeky bitch.
I closed my eyes, and I felt a gush of air against my face and then a winding blow to my chest.

My eyes were tightly closed, but it didn't stop the tears pouring out of them. No noise left my lips though.

Had my dad just kicked his twelve-year-old daughter while she was lying on the floor! Mum ran into the living room screaming at him to leave me alone, but I think that made him even angrier and he started screaming and shouting in my mum's face, she wasn't taking any of it.

'One fucking day Jason, one fucking day you have been home, and already you are starting this shit again' dad went to speak, but she spoke over him
'you promised this was a fresh start for all of us, didn't you' she shouted,

'I don't know what wrong with me' he said holding onto his head.

He sat down on the sofa and mum told me to go upstairs. As I got myself up off the floor, I could see dad rocking backward and forwards in the chair, clenching hold of big clumps of hair on each side of his head.

'Please I don't know what is wrong with me.'

'What are you talking about?' mum had asked.

'I don't know, please I can't do this' was all that my dad repeated.

I had been in the house for less than an hour, and already he had kicked me. I should have known better than to answer him back, but I didn't care anymore. I sat in my room and got out my journal and started writing my thoughts down, it was the only way I could feel in control, I needed to talk to someone, but that wasn't going ever to happen, not if my life was worth living.

Dad had threatened to kill me, and I believed him, so my journal became the only way I could express myself. I wished my life away on that paper, hoping I could just get away from it all, but I knew that last time I tried to run away, it caused me more hassle than it was worth. knowing I had no control over my life became something I just had to learn to accept.

Hospital Trip Number Two...

      It was a few days after my dad had kicked me, and to be fair, he had seemed sorry and was acting all nice around me. I was sat in the living room on the sofa, and the twins were lying on the floor with coloring books. Top of the pops two was on the television, it was Sunday afternoon, and mum was cooking dinner in the kitchen. Dad was reading his paper at the table on the other side of the room, as usual, he always read the newspaper backward, starting with the football scores and making his way back to the headlines.

'Dinners ready in five' mum shouted though

'Okay' came three replies from the living room.

As I went to get up I had a familiar sharp pain in the groin of my leg; I couldn't move. Daniel started laughing at me, and Callum ran into the kitchen.
My dad was the first person to come into the living room, and he asked me what was wrong. I explained as best as I could through the pain that it was like last time I needed an operation

'Are you sure you're not acting a little over the top?' he asked,

'You can tell she isn't' my mum replied from behind him and she walked into the hall and grabbed her coat.

'Where the fuck are you going?' dad snapped at her

'To use Amy's phone for fuck sake; I won't be a minute.'

The ambulance was quick to be fair to them; I was in the hospital for ten days altogether.
I did have a strangulated hernia again but to be on the safe side the surgeon decided to place a camera inside me through an incursion under my belly button just to make sure I didn't get another hernia. If any had been left behind, it could have poisoned my body. As they were looking around my insides with this tiny camera they noticed my appendix was in desperate need of removing, it had inflamed so much that the toxic acids were burning the outer layer of my appendix wall.

When I woke up I felt dizzy and struggled to keep my eyes open, I heard my mums voice, but I didn't see her. She was telling me to go back to sleep, and I must have drifted off.

The next time I woke, it was in the middle of the night, the lights were off in my room, but the walls were glass, so the lights from the corridor shined brightly enough. I turned my head towards the sound I heard beside me, almost like a quiet washing machine, this big grey machine was towering over me.

I had seen tubes with red stuff running through them and realized it was blood; it was my blood. I had been put on dialyzes to clean out my blood just in case any toxins had got into my blood. I didn't know this at the time and fell back to sleep.

The next morning the nurse had explained that there were complications and that I had almost died on the operating table, she said I was lucky I had a common blood group of O positive and that some of the blood going back into my body was someone else

'Does that mean I'm not me?' I asked, she looked at me and giggled and then told me I was funny, but most of all very brave.

I lay there feeling chuffed with myself, I spent most of the day on my own drifting in and out of sleep, after nine days of rest I could return home. The hospital was a welcome break, even if it meant that I was celebrating my 13th birthday in a hospital bed.

I didn't mind, and mum had come to visit me with the twins. She told me I had more presents at home, but it turned out that they couldn't afford much more than a few small trinkets and a new top.

I was happy enough and could have stayed in that hospital, even though I was in pain throughout most of my stay, I was safe for a brief time at least.

I couldn't wait to get back to school, I had spent most of the summer holidays in my bedroom because of my operation, and then when I was okay; there was always a reason I had pissed my dad off, and he had grounded me. This hadn't gone unnoticed though, my auntie Amy started to ask questions, and I think my mum had started to confide in her about how strict dad was with me, and to be fair, how he was beginning to take out his frustrations on the twins as well. Amy and Pat had started coming to our house more often. Amy had offered to take me to hers to give dad a break from me, that annoyed me so much, but I learned to bite my tongue.

She finally got her own way the weekend before I was due to back to school, I was stopping overnight and sleeping in my aunt's room, I must have been dreaming because I woke up to the soft sound her voice calling my name.

I opened my eyes, and it was dark, apparently the middle of the night, Amy was standing above me.

'Sarah, it's okay, you're okay.'

'Sarah, you are safe now love' she said as I sat up.

The next morning, I had woken up later than everyone else in the house, I could hear them all downstairs in the kitchen, laughing and giggling to each other. Walking onto the landing Mitzie nearly tripped me up getting under my legs; Mitzie was one of Amy's five dogs, she also had four Siamese cats. They used to hiss at me a lot, but her dogs were friendly, especially Monty. He always wanted a fuss.

Sat at the top of the stairs I could hear my aunt talking to the girls, 'Do you think Sarah has been acting weird lately?'
'Isn't she always weird,' answered Sally

'No, I meant quiet and withdrawn maybe. I don't think all in rosy at home' Amy had replied, her tone of voice seemed worrisome.

'Huh, rosy at home, Uncle Jas has never been the rosiest of characters anyway, I sure you are worrying about nothing mum' Veronica said sarcastically.

Monty then darted down the stairs wagging his tail; he had heard Amy kick his bowl. So, off he went as fast as his little paws would take him.
I just sat down on the top step looking through the gaps in the banister wishing I had a life more like them. Amy's girls seemed to have it all, anything they wanted they got unless they had been badly behaved which was usually stealing or getting into a fight at school.

She must have noticed me sat there and called me downstairs, but I shook my head and went back into the room I had slept in.

Amy followed me up the stairs, I was sure she was going to tell me off for ignoring her but instead she walked into the room told me to stand up and put her arms around me.

'We need to talk' she said, I just nodded my head, and she smiled back at me.

'First, I need a cup of tea, wait here I will be back in five minutes,

I looked back up at her a smiled, but I wasn't in the mood for talking. I was tired and fed up, and no amount of talking could change that, and I think it must have shown as she went to walk out the room and she turned to me and said

'We do need to talk you know? I will be back in a minute; do you want anything?

'No thank you' I replied.

I sat on her bed, my heart started pumping, and I knew what questions she wanted to ask me, it was obvious what she wanted to know from the way she was acting. Five minutes seemed more like half an hour and the longer I sat in her room waiting to be questioned the harder my heart would beat, this caused me sharp shooting pains just below my breastbone and shoulder blades.

It would make me have to calm my worrying down, I knew my heart was a bit dodgy and forgot to beat sometimes, but that chest pain always worried me.

What happens if it just forgets to beat completely? It would just be my luck I thought to myself. Amy walked back into the bedroom.

'You okay' she asked,

'Yes, thank you I am fine, just a bit of a tight chest that's all.' I reassured her

'Your mother needs to take you to the bloody doctors; you seem to be getting this tightness a lot lately.' She snapped 'Sorry it's not your fault, your mother winds me up sometimes'.

I just wanted the whole conversation to hurry up and end 'What did you want to talk about?' I asked, but deep down I knew exactly what she want to talk about.

'Your father.'

I was annoyed,

'What do you mean my father? I snapped.

'I know how he treats you, Sarah, I have eyes dear, and he has told me everything, but I need to hear it from you.' She said, 'do you understand?'

I understood completely what she meant, or at least I thought I did, I thought it was strange that dad had told his sister about abusing me, yet she didn't seem to mind. Maybe just needed the words to come out of my own mouth before she could believe it.
So, I took a deep breath and started telling her about the abuse and the things my dad was forcing me to do. I looked up at her, and the look on her face said it all, I burst into tears cupping my head in my hands.

'It's okay, I am listening' she said,
So, I carried on telling her everything; I had snot dripping
down my nose and tears streaming down my face. I felt
Amy get up from the bed beside me, so I looked up at her.
She was now standing up and shaking her head.

'Do you know how evil someone must be to make up sick
and perverse lies like that?'

I couldn't believe it.
The state I was in trying to confess my secret, and she
didn't believe me at all.
I begged her and told her I was telling the truth, but she
just repeated that I must be sick to come out with lies like
that. I was still begging her to believe me when she
laughed straight in my face and walked towards the door.

'God help you when your dad hears what you are saying
about him, I think you need medical help love, I think you
should have been the one in hospital, not him.' She
smirked at me and continued 'you sent him to that looney
bin, y'know that it was you and that poison mouth off
yours, you disgust me, you really do.'

With that she walked out of the room, I heard her
footsteps walk halfway down the stairs, and she stopped,
then the steps carried on until she was down stairs. I lay
on the bed for about an hour crying before I had fallen to
sleep. I dreamt of a man trying to kill me; this wasn't the
first time I had, had this dream.

*I am at Bonny's caravan site in Newcastle, with all my family
apart from my dad, we are all walking into town, a big gang of
us. My cousin's arm in arm and the adults all chatting to
themselves.*

I am walking at the back, and a red butterfly catches my eye. So, being me, I turn to follow the butterflies trail with my eyes and when I turn back round all the chatting has stopped, and I realize I am on my own. My family is nowhere to be seen, I started walking faster down the road to catch up, hoping that when I turned the corner, I would catch up with them, but as I got to the bottom of the lane the streets were deserted, and the clouds had darkened.

Carrying on toward to seafront and still no sign of them, looking hopelessly in the arcades and cafes that lined the streets but still no signal. I had noticed a small middle-aged man walking toward me, for some reason he made me feel uneasy, so I crossed to the road. I had hoped to find my family on the beach, but it was empty, which seemed weird as it was the height of the summer and usually the beach was full of tourists and locals enjoying the sun. I had a sense that someone was behind me and when I turned around, I saw the middle-aged man staring at me. His eyes were as dark.

Suddenly a long cold shiver ran down my spine like a surge of electricity running through me. Something told me to run, so I turned around and ran towards the arcades again.
Once I entered the amusement, i could see that the lights were on. All the different sounds of the rides and the games machines filled the air, but not one single person was in there.

I turned to walk back toward the door, but the man was now standing in the doorway, he didn't speak, he just stared right through me. Then I watched as his face started to distort, and his features were changing, molding into one another, he seemed to be getting smaller too.

I was hoping he was dying or something. I just froze, fixated on the changing man in front of me. I blinked once, and then again as my eyes started to play tricks on me.

My Life in His Hands

The old man had turned into my dad, he looked like him in every single way, but his eyes weren't my dad's eyes. They were almost black with no pupil to be seen. I turned to run, hiding behind a gambling machine and hoping whatever it was that changed into my dad would leave me alone. I crouched down into a ball covering my face with my arm and my knees but heard something close to me, as I looked up. My dad was stood above me with a knife in his hands, I institutively kicked out at him as I tried to scurry back to get away, I could see the door, and people were walking past the front of the arcade I tried to shout, but no noise would come out of me.

My dad was lunging towards me with the knife, but I am too quick for him to catch, I must have hurt his leg as I kicked out because he was limping towards me now. I see a tall umbrella by the entrance to the toilets, it was only a few yards away, but for some reason I seemed to be pinned to the floor, all I could do was crawl away from him. It was like gravity was keeping me low to the ground. As I got closer to the umbrella, I felt my dad grab hold of my ankle and pull me towards him. I dragged myself back towards the umbrella stand, as he lunged towards my chest with the knife, I managed to open the umbrella and held it in front of me almost like a shield, the force of his weight falling on the umbrella almost pierced my skin, as the knife came down with him. The metal spear on the end of the umbrella went straight through his chest, the creature was changing again, his features distorted revealing the middle-aged man, but his eyes were somehow kinder, they had gone from deep dark blue, almost black color into a pale sky blue, he smiles before closing his eyes....

And then I woke up; I always wake up at the same time, every time I have had this dream.

I lay in my bed looking up at the ceiling, thinking about my dream, over and over again. I am suddenly snapped out of my daydream with the sound of Naomi running on the landing just outside my room. She was shouting downstairs to Vee; her voice had startled me.

I didn't want to go downstairs I was worried about what Amy would say, but as I listened intently, I heard my mum talking, so I decided to go wants anyway. I walked back over to my made-up bed and started to get dressed as I made my way to the bathroom to have a wash I could hear my mum and Amy walking into the kitchen.

When I got downstairs she was making my mum a cup of tea and Granny had just walked in through the front door; mum was sat at the kitchen table with a fag hanging out of her mouth.

I waited a few seconds as Granny walked into the kitchen and she must have noticed me walking down the stairs, she just smiled at me and started talking to Amy about a job she needed my uncle to do. Everything seemed normal, and it would be a while before the subject with my Auntie Amy would come up again.

Blossoming Friendships...

I had been in the second year of St Dominic's for a few weeks, and when you're in the second year you feel a bit more appreciated, you are no longer the new kid. I remember one day sat in an assembly like we had to do every week, but I had stuck into the hall late, I was in the toilets having a makeup malfunction. Most of my mates did their makeup at home, but my dad would have killed me if he had seen me even wearing a shiny lip gloss. So, as I tried to creep into the hall one of the teachers seen me and ushered me just to sit down.

Stacey was sat near the end of the row, so I squeezed in beside her, she elbowed me in the ribs and smiled. I elbowed her back, and we heard the teacher at the back hushing, we just giggled silently covering our mouths with our hands. The assembly was so dull I wasn't taking any of it in, I was too busy thinking about what song I should sing in the talent show coming up a few weeks later when I felt a tap on my shoulder, I turned around at two boys were giggling to themselves.

The one was quite tall, with mousy blond hair and the other boy was tiny like me with dark hair. I looked at Stacey shaking my head, and I felt the tapping again this time on my opposite shoulder. I turned right around in my chair and looked back at the sniggering boys.

'Why are you tapping me?' I asked,

'Why are you tapping me' the taller boy said trying to put on my English accent

'Excuse me' said the small dark-haired boy 'Are you forgetting I lived in England too?' He asked his mate, who now looked sheepish and uncomfortable.

Later, in the day I had bumped into Stacey in the corridor, she told me the lad tapping me was called Dylan and that he was asking loads of questions about me.

'Like what?' I asked

'y'know just things like, where do you live, whose class you are in, oh and he did ask if you had a boyfriend' she said smiling

'What did you say?'

I wanted to know every detail, but one of the office staff had seen us and told us to get to class; Stacey and I had arranged to meet each other and lunch and started walking separate way to get to our classes

'He's in my next lesson, shall I tell him you like him' she shouted to me

'No, I don't know him' I replied.

I could help but think about his cheeky little smile, and his sparkling hazel eyes. I had been thinking about him most of my math's lesson, and I have no idea what we were meant to be doing. As my lesson finished, I realized I hadn't written anything in my exercise book. At that point, I had to admit to myself that the boy in the hall was cute. His smile was so endearing, and he stuck up for me when his friend was taking the mick out of me, and that wasn't something I was used to.

Later, at lunchtime I found myself trying to find Stacey to see if she had said anything to the boy who caught my eye, I walked out of the dining hall after not really touching any of my food. I wasn't in the mood to eat and just needed to see my mate before I went out of my mind, I was feeling very vulnerable at that point. No boy had ever taken an interest in me. I was scared and nervous but just needed to know what she had said to him in her lesson. The anticipation was increasing as I walked down the hard stone steps towards the all-weather pitch at the front of the school. When I got to the bottom I saw Stacey and the other girls sat on the steps, they were watching the boys playing football, most of the lads were all in older years to us, but they loved the attention the first and second-year girls gave them.
So, they started to show off. It was a warm summers afternoon, and some of the boys were playing with their tops off, trying to show off their pale Irish skin.

Stacey liked a boy in the last year, she looked older than most of the girls her age, but Tommy was with a girl in year ten, and he wasn't that interested in her, or at least he acted like he didn't notice her. Suzanne was slumped on the steps as if all the wind had been taken out of her.

'What up with you?' I asked,

'Just boys' she said looking over to the boys playing football at the far end of the piths

'Who needs boys' I said as reassuringly as I could, before sitting down beside her

'It's okay for you Sarah; you have someone who likes you.'

'Oh, yeah sure I do' I replied sarcastically

'Dylan has been asking about you all morning; it's starting to do my head in' she snapped.

'Well sorry,' I said getting up. 'I didn't ask anyone to like me, did I? And don't worry I'm sure Dylan won't like me once he gets to know me anyway.' I snapped back.

'I am sick and tired of you always putting yourself down, you are pretty and funny, and I can see why he might like you, but no Sarah isn't good enough. It's fucking stupid, you are fucking stupid' she looked at me the whole time while saying it, but I just looked away and stared down at the floor.
'Well if that's how you feel' I said with tears in my eyes and walked away.

The girls walked over to her to ask what had happened, they all loved a bit of gossip, and as usual, I was the topic of conversation, the school was shit I remember thinking to myself. In a mood and wanting to be left on my own, I made my way towards the back of the school behind the canteen.

There was an old areophane hanger where the hard nuts of the class used to hang out and get stoned, I didn't smoke, but I just wanted to be as far away from Stacey as possible. I could see the hanger was full of lads, so I decided to sit on the field beside it, I was just daydreaming, and was honestly feeling sorry for myself, after all, I was nothing but a dirty whore as far as my dad was concerned. Tears started forming in my eyes, and I was angry as the emotion began running down my cheeks, if anyone had seen me crying I would have been picked on, or they would have asked questions, so I wiped my face and made my way to the girl's toilets. When I got to the bathrooms, there was a group of year one girls in the toilets smoking.

I squeezed past them to get into the cubical, and a small blonde-haired girl piped up 'Oh, dickhead, don't push past.'

'Why don't you just fuck off' I replied.

The blonde girl laughed with her friends, and they were all giggling at me with my red puffed up eyes from crying.

'Oh, you English bitch, don't month me or I'll beat the living shit out of you' she said walking towards me.

I closed the cubical door and sat on the closed toilet seat with my feet up in front of me. I could hear the girls kicking the door from the other side

'Leave me alone' I shouted,

'I will leave you alone if you come out and fight bubbles' one of the other girls said,

'Yeah come out bitch I want to paint the floor with you face you English cow' bubbles said.

I'm not sure what the blonde girl's real name was, but I now knew her as Bubbles. Eventually, they left as the bell went for the end of lunch.
I sat there waiting for the coast to be clear before I decided to head to class, I had Art in my next lesson, and we were being taught how to do shading using different pencils, I had been looking forward to drawing and loved anything that let me be creative.

I arrived at class a few minutes late, but my teacher just hurried me to my chair.

My art class had lasted just over an hour, and it was the last break, we only had a fifteen-minute break. I decided to stay behind in class and continue with my work. Mrs. Burman who was my art teacher, came across to my table after the rest of the pupils had left the classroom.

'Do you want to help me with a project? She asked.

She explained that we were doing a piece for the main hall, demonstrating the talents of our year group; I was pleased that she asked me.

'Of course, I will' I said excitedly.

'I will explain more in your next lesson' she smiled at me, and she left the room.
I just sat at my table and carried on with my work, I was good at drawing, and it was probably the only thing I was confident about at that point in my life. After the bell had gone to tell us it was the end of our break time. I made my way out of the classroom. I had P.E last lesson, but I had told my teacher that I felt ill, so she sent me to the back of the P.E hall with some worksheets about keeping healthy using sport.

I didn't read the sheet, which showed at the end of the lesson when my teacher had asked if had finished the worksheet. I told her that I felt too sick to concentrate and she seemed to believe me, while the girls were getting changed I was told to wait in the corridor while the rest of the class finished getting ready.
As I stood in the hallway, I saw a few boys walking around with a clipboard. One of the boys was Dylan's friend that he was sitting beside that morning.

'My mate likes you' he said smirking.

'I'm sure he does' I replied, believing that no boy would ever like me, why would they I was a dirty slag after all.

'Honestly' he said, 'he thinks you are cute and wants to meet up sometime' he said.

Still feeling insecure and worried it was just a trap to take the piss out of me, even more, I replied

'Tell Dylan if he likes me, he should have the balls to tell me himself, if not then he obviously doesn't like me that much eh?'

'The boy looked at me and smiled. 'I like you, your pretty cool and straight to the point' he said. 'I will tell him, but he does like you. Do you have a boyfriend?' he asked as he walked away.

I shook my head, 'Cool I will tell him' he said before I had a chance to reply he had run up the corridor to catch up with his mates.

'Great' I said out loud.
On the way home is seen Stacey walking ahead of me. Usually, I would have run to catch up with her, but I was still pissed off with the way she was with me at lunchtime. I heard footsteps behind me, and I turned around expecting to see bubbles running towards me, but it was Dylan, with that big smile, he crunched his nose as he got closer. I smiled back at him as he stood beside me panting, apparently out of breath.

'Hello, my names Dylan.'

'I know' I replied, 'Stacey told me.'

'And you are Sarah, is that right? 'He asked. I nodded my head, and we started walking up the road.

'You live near me, don't you?' I asked.

'Yeah I live in the same square as Stacey' he replied still with a big grin on his face.

I had explained where I lived, and we arranged to meet up with each other later in the day.

I spent a lot of time with Dylan over the next few weeks, and we seemed to get on well. One day on a Saturday afternoon, Dylan and I were sat on top of the 'fairy hill' as everyone called it.
The big hill was situated at the top end of our estate; it was a steep grassy hill leading down to the Community Centre, we were just talking about random shit when Dylan turned to me and said
'So, are you, my girlfriend, now? His voice sounded nervous, I looked at him and giggled.

I didn't mean to, and I instantly felt terrible when I had seen the look on his poor face, I didn't mean to hurt his feeling, but I couldn't tell I had by to look in his eyes.

'I'm sorry I shouldn't have laughed, it's a nervous thing I do.'

I looked him straight in the eyes, and that cheeky smile formed back on his face.

'I just didn't expect anyone to like me that way' I said concerning.

I knew he was genuine, but a small part of me was worried he would have laughed at me if I had answered yes.

'Of course, I like you' he said sliding my hair from the front of my face, so I could see him. He smiled at me and stroked my hair. 'Look at you, what's not to like?' he said as he placed his arm around me and cuddled me into his chest.

'So, is that a yes?' he asked,

'That's a yes' I assured him.

Unwanted Attention...

Life at home was as bad as ever, dad was still abusing me when mum was out at work, and the boys were in bed, dad had also started getting heavier handed with the twins, they were getting badly behave, and even though they were twins, you wouldn't have thought it. Callum was a blonde hair blue eyed little boy with pale skin, whereas Daniel was dark haired, green eyes and had a natural tan to his skin. There was a family joke that Callum was swapped at birth because he looked nothing like any of us. Callum took this to heart, like with most things, but that was silly because if our dad had known something annoyed you, he would keep doing it till you went moody and then you could guarantee a good telling off would follow. The twin's appearance wasn't the only things that were opposite with them.

They couldn't agree on anything which always led to them arguing and hitting each other, and they would drive mum furious and never listened to a word she ever said to them. If mum smacked Callum, it was the end of the world, but if Daniel got a smack, he would argue back at her and usually laugh in her face. I admired that he had no fear, but at the same time, I doubted he had to cope with the shit thrown at me all the time.

Sometimes he would argue so severely that our mum would lose it with him.

I remember one day she lost her temper, Daniel had been pushing her all day long, and dad was out. I don't recall where he was.

Mum had grabbed the wooden spoon off the kitchen side, after smacking him once hadn't worked she pulled his pants down and slapped him repeatedly with the spoon. Daniel was laughing at her a goading her 'it doesn't hurt' he kept saying every time she made contact with his bare bum, he pushed and pushed. Eventually, the wooden spoon snapped. His bum was red raw, but he still laughed in her face, she pushed him to the ground and stormed out of the house. Luckily, I was well behaved, and Mum never really needed to tell me off.

Sometimes I would get screamed and shouted at for saying the wrong thing at the wrong time, but that was only if the twins had pushed her to her limits, most of the time she was fine with me, and we would even have a laugh when it was just us in the house.

Mum had been out of the house for about half an hour; Daniel had started to cry when she walked out of the house and had now fallen asleep on the sofa, Callum was playing in his room. Matthew must have been out with dad because he wasn't at home, and I was in the kitchen when there was a knock at the front door. As I walked into the hall, Callum came running down.

'Callum, can you go upstairs and play please?' I asked, he just smiled at me and sat on the third step from the top and he was looking at me through the banister, his eyes and nose scrunched up as he tried his hardest to give me an evil look.

'Go upstairs' I repeated, but he just stared at me.
The door knocked again, and as I opened it I saw Dylan stood waiting for me

'Are you still coming out?' he asked.

'I can't' I explained 'mum has just stormed off and I don't know where she is, so I have been left with the twins again'

You could see with the disappointed look his face, that he wanted me to come out, but I couldn't leave the twins.

'Joy of having shit parents eh? I said.

We sat outside in the front garden and just spent time chatting, we both had the same star sign, and one of the most prominent traits were that we both talked a lot, which was brilliant, we never had a dull moment together because there was always lots of things to discuss.
Some days little conversations could keep us occupied for hours on end, we would just keep bouncing off each other. It's strange, even though he was younger than me and we had only known each other a matter of months, when we were together, I felt safe, like almost protected.

Dylan had no idea about the secrets that happened behind that front door, and I had planned to keep it that way. He seemed to like me for being me, and when I was around him, I could just act like an ordinary thirteen-year-old girl. I didn't have to be a big sister or pretend to be a mum for dad's sake, I could just be me, even if I weren't a hundred percent sure how I was meant to act, this boy liked me the way I was, and that was good enough for me.

We had been talking and cuddling on the front doorstep for about half an hour when mum had finally returned home. She didn't look stressed anymore and explained that she had gone to Auntie Amy's to calm down. I didn't blame her, my brother had pushed her that day and I was slightly surprised when he heard her talking to me out the front, he squeezed past Dylan and me and ran towards mum with his arms up for a hug.

She picked him up and hugged him while doing so she explained that he was very poorly behaved and kissed him on the forehead before putting him back down.

'Should we go back in?' mum looked at me

'Can I get out, for an hour?' I asked,

'No but Dylan can come in, your dad is due home with Matthew anytime soon.'

'But why has that got anything to do with me?' I replied.

'Sarah please' she looked at me with a concerning look

'I don't mind, we can chill inside' Dylan said as he stood up.

We were sat in the living room while the twins were arguing upstairs above us, my mum was pottering about in the kitchen. Dylan and I were watching some rubbish on the TV, but I couldn't tell you what we were watching because I was just waiting for something to happen. In the living room was a three-seater sofa and a two-seater, Dylan and I were sat on the two-seaters together, my head resting on his shoulder and my feet tucked up beside me, just then I heard my dad coming in through the front door. I sat up straight and put my legs down.

'I guess you aren't allowed your feet on the furniture' he asked.

I grinned at his confused looking face, 'Something like that'

We were sat beside each other when dad walked in the room with Matthew in his arms, he placed him on the floor in front of the television, and he looked up at Dylan and me with a grin on his face. We sat there feeling slightly uncomfortable and just looked at each other; dad sat on the other sofa and reached for the remote to turn the television over. I and Dylan both sat with our arms closed, I moved closer to him.

I guessed my dad hadn't noticed, we were holding hands but hoping we wouldn't be seen. Thinking back, we were both quite shy and embarrassed, but my dad had noticed.

'You can sit there trying to hold hands as much as you like' he continued 'you know when I was a kid I used to do the same thing, my girl and I at the time would sit just like you two.'

'Leave them alone Jason' mum shouted from the kitchen.

Dylan stayed for dinner and went home shortly afterward. Mum had said that he seemed nice and dad just took the piss out of me; he asked what the poor sod would see in me.

I was upset obviously and ran upstairs to my bedroom. It was only about six in the evening, but I went straight to bed. I didn't want to be downstairs, and I knew I wasn't allowed out, so I got undressed and sat in bed with my journal, I used to write all my feeling down in this little book as you can imagine all the pent up anger inside me was put into words and placed on the paper, you could see from my hand writing that when I first open the book I am full of rage, the pen marks are thick and bold, as the page continues and I calm down my handwriting gets neater and softer. The last line in my journal that night read

'I hate living this life; **I just want to take this pain** away and feel like a real person, until then my life is *in HIS hands*. The monster I call my father. He has made my life hell since the day I met him. I *__hate__* him and *always will.*'

I closed my book and placed it back underneath my mattress, and rearranged my sheet before I climbed back into bed, I was asleep but seven o'clock that night. I always feel better after having a rant on paper.

The next day I went over to Claire's house, but she was out with her mum shopping.
Claire's dad had invited me in to wait as it was raining outside, not that it was anything new, in Northern Ireland it seemed to rain most of the time growing up. I decided it was better to wait indoors than be seen by my dad waiting in the rain. My kitchen doors faced Claire's row of houses, and I usually see him starring out of them.

I was sat in the living room waiting and feeling really on edge. Claire's dad was the only person in the house, and he made a comment about my hair being down for a change and that it made me look older.

I thought it was weird him saying that because I have never been told, I looked older. I was small, petite and I might have been thirteen but to look at me, you would have guessed I was about ten or maybe eleven years old. He sat in a chair opposite me and kept staring at me.

'You have wonderful eyes' he said in his creepy voice.
'Very green, wonderful eyes' he stood up.
'oh, wait or are the brown?'

He started walking closer to me with his head to one side; I felt like he was examining my face or something. I felt so uncomfortable as he stood towering over me.

'What color would you say they were?' he asked

'Err, I, I think they are hazel' I replied my voice slightly shaky.

My gut was telling me to get away so; I tried to make an excuse to go home. I said that my tea would be ready soon and went to get up from my seat.

'No point in leaving so soon, Claire will be back shortly, keep me company please!' he asked.

'I really should go' I said trying to push past him.

He stayed towering over me and not letting me leave, asking me if I was still a virgin and wanting to know what I get up to with my boyfriend. The front door opens, and the sleazy man backs away from me. I cannot tell you how grateful I am to see Claire walking in. I felt like I was about to cry and, so I made my excuses to leave. 'Have I done something wrong?' she asked concerned.

'No, I just need to get back I have been waiting for ages, and you know what my dad's like' I said.

We said our goodbyes and I walked back home across the road towards my back gate.

When I walked up towards the back door I could see dad sitting at the kitchen table; he looked pissed off but this time more than usual.

My Life in His Hands

As I got closer I could see he was holding something in his hands; it was my journal. That explained the evil looks he was giving me, I walked through the patio door and closed it behind me, I turned to look at my dad, waiting for him to explode, but instead, he just stared straight through me with that piercing evil stare.

I walked closer to the kitchen table and looked down at my journal in his hands, his fingertips were white from the force he was squeezing the book.

'Is that mine?' I asked trying to break the silence.

His stare hadn't moved away from the wall where I was just stood; I was unsure if he heard me, so I repeated the question.

'Dad is that my book?'

I made a point of speaking a little louder, his head turned to look at me, but his body stayed stiff, his fingers still squeezing the life out of my book.

'I made your life hell!' he shouted 'I made your fucking pointless life hell! You don't even know the meaning.' He started to get up from his chair and slammed the book on the table, keeping his left palm flat on top of the cover.

'You silly little bitch' he continued, his hand moved off my book, and he started to saunter towards me, I cowered up against the wall,

'Please daddy' I begged.

'I have made your life hell for thirteen years, have I? You have made my life hell since the second you were born, I should have slit your neck when I had the chance!' he screamed in my face.

'You haven't known me since I was born' I muttered.

I knew I shouldn't have answered him back but couldn't help myself. Dad stood up, pushing the table to one side and squared up to me, spraying his rotten saliva all over my face, his dirty, smoky breath warm against my skin. He was looking at me as if he was waiting for an apology, but I just looked him dead in the face.

That apparently angered him more as he punched me in the stomach, he then stepped back, forcing my body to stand upright. Then he just stood there and watched me sobbing.

After a moment of gloating, he turned to pick up my book that was still on the table and threw it at me.
It bounced off the side of my shoulder and then fell to the floor, breaking the binder as it hit the ground with force.

'You are stupid if you think I will let you own a diary' he said.

His tone was calm as he sat back down at the table

'Why do you even think I would let you write some diseased lies on paper? You are sick Sarah! Who else have you told?' He asked.

'No one I have never told anyone, please dad I promised you I wouldn't, didn't I?' I pleaded.

'Well I don't believe you' he replied,

'I promise you, dad, I haven't ever told anyone, and I swear I won't, ever.' I continued 'I shouldn't have written those things I was angry, I'm sorry dad please dad I'm sorry.'

I was begging and sobbing, leaning back into the wall. My arm was warm to touch and throbbing where the corner of the book had hit me.

'Your mum will be home soon, get upstairs in my room, I will be up in a minute' he said getting back up of his chair.

'Fucking move now!' he shouted.

I knew only too well what that meant. I was stood in my dad room, tears rolling down my face.

I heard him lock the front door and then I heard his footsteps coming up the stairs, my heart started beating to the rhythm of the steps, then he opened the door. Dad already had his trousers off when he walked in the bedroom. He told me to get on my knees and show him how sorry I was.

Ironic really, I had left Claire's house to get away from her monster of a dad, and I walked straight back into the lion's den where my monster was waiting for me.

All this at the age of twelve, could my life get any worse? Well, I was about to find out.

Me and My Big Mouth...

Saint Dominic's was not a bad school, all in all. The girls were so bitchy it was unbelievable, you had to be there to understand. I was in P.E one day and at the end of the lesson we were forced to have showers, I never really had a shower, I kept my underwear on, under my towel, and just wet my hair and shoulders. Some girls were a lot more confident than me, apart from the fact that my body was covered in scars and bruises; I was nowhere near as developed as most of the girls in my year. I was tiny, with a petite frame and completely flat chested, most of the girls in the shower, had women's bodies already at the age of twelve and thirteen. I looked at them with envy and one girl Shannon had noticed me looking in their direction.

'Owe what are you looking at?' she is asking.

'Nothing, I'm sorry' I said looking away, I hadn't seen her walk close to me I just felt her rip my towel off me.

I tried to get it back, but she was stronger than me, she passed my towel back to her friend and stood naked in front of me, I looked away.

'You little girl bless, look you don't even have any boobies' she said mocking me.

'Leave me alone' I shouted,

'Or you will do what exactly' she replied.

I ran out of the shower almost slipping as my wet feet contacted the slippery floor, grabbing my clothes as fast as I could I ran towards the toilet on the other end of the changing rooms. As I sat holding my now damp uniform, in my arms I heard the group of girls leaving the shower; they were all giggling and making fun of me.

'Did you see her body?' One girl asked,

'I know, that big burn on her leg looks like she been put on a fucking cooker or something' her friend replied,

'I did hear he dad beats the fuck out of her.'

The rage was burning inside me as I heard them gossiping about me, I was angrier than upset. As I put my clothes on I could hear them still hear them mocking me, I stormed out of the toilet cubical and walked straight up to the blond-haired girl who pulled my towel off.

'You know fuck all' I shouted in her face, my blood was boiling. 'The burn on my leg is my fucking birthmark, not a burn, why don't you ask me questions before you start trying to find the answers eh?'
I stood back and looked at her; she smirked at me

'Aye well I think you are full of shite' she turned around to continue laughing with her friends.

I was so angry, and I pulled her over her shoulder, forcing her to face me. 'Like I said you know fuck all.'

'I know you are gonna get your shit kicked in after school, silly cow. Even Bubbles is going to beat the clean shit out of you, and I will be stood there laughing, what are you going to do then?' she asked.

I just turned and walked towards the entrance to the P.E hall. I needed to get away before I lost it, standing outside the changing room was my P.E teacher talking to my art teacher, both women looked on edge when they noticed me stood there.

'Sarah gets back into the changing rooms now' she ordered, so I just folded my arms as if to stand my ground,

'I refuse to go back in there, miss. The girls are horrible to me' I said in an almost needy and weak voice.

'Grow up and get back to class' she ordered again, but I just kept walking towards the other side of the hall. 'Sarah Rosmond, I am not going to tell you again, go back to class or go on detention' she said,

'Detention it is then' I replied with a grin on my face, I walked out of the hall and went straight towards the fire exit at the side of the school. Once I was outside, I had decided I wasn't going back to school, I had a few hours to kill, so I walked back towards Ballymore, but I took the back route, through the fields and past the U.S.P.C.A Building on the top of the hill.

I sat on the wall outside for a while, admiring the dogs playing peacefully in the big locked up compound, the dogs seemed happy enough, but I started to think about how it somehow mirrored my situation and just because the dogs seemed happy enough, didn't mean they were. I knew only too well how to act like I was okay, or to pretend that I wasn't scared. I also felt like I was locked up, not in the same way as these dogs but the sense that I had no control of my own life in any way.

Mum didn't have any control either, but my life was in my dad's hands, and I felt like he could get away with anything. I started to daydream about how I could help the dogs escape and maybe that would somehow make it easier for me to escape from my life at home, but every scenario had a lousy ending.

When I finally returned home, I saw all the curtains drawn, and I was a little apprehensive as I opened the front door. The whole house was dark, and silent, which wasn't normal. The twins were always home from school by now, I looked down at my watch, worried that I had got back too early, but it was three thirty, the same time I got home every day.

I closed the door behind me as quietly as possible and crept into the kitchen expecting my mum to be out and my dad to be asleep but as I opened the kitchen door, I saw my dad pacing the length of the kitchen muttering to himself. He hadn't noticed me walk past him as I headed straight for the living room, which was also dark. I went towards the curtains to open them, but I heard my mum behind me,

'Don't open them' she said firmly

'Why?' I asked,

'Do you want to start him off again?'

I just looked at her and glanced towards the kitchen where he was still pacing backward and forwards, muttering random words which might have made sense in his head but to us, it was just a rumbling noise.

'You need to go upstairs and stay there pleased' mum had said

'But what have I done wrong' I asked, looking at her with tears in my eyes.

Usually, if I was sent to my bedroom looking mum, I knew to expect a beating off my dad when he would come upstairs eventually to see why I had been told off, some days he would play on it and leave me for hours before he would come and find me.

It was like a little game to him, and he loved seeing the fear in my eyes, the longer I was waiting, the harsher the telling off would be, so I didn't want to be sent to my room. Plus, I tried to spend as little time upstairs as possible, that's where most of the sexual abuse would take place, and I felt safer when I was down the stairs with mum and the boys.

'Please mum' I pleaded.

'Have you told anyone about him?' she asked nodding in my dad direction, which was still in a world of his own.

'What do you mean?' I asked confused

'You know what I fucking mean, just go upstairs; I will be up in a few minutes, please.'

She was almost begging me, so I knew it was terrible whatever the reason for the atmosphere in the house.

When I went up to my room I seen all the curtains in the whole house had been drawn closed, I hadn't dared open my curtains, so I put my light on and started to read through my homework that was due in a few days later.

About an hour had passed before I heard any movement on the stairs, I heard footsteps getting closer to my bedroom door, so I closed my English books and placed them back in my bag, as I turned to look towards my door, mum was stood with tears in her eyes.
'I think you need to go straight to bed' she said,

'But it's early, and I haven't had dinner yet?' I replied

'I am not cooking when he is in this mood; I suggest you go to sleep and quick before he comes up the stairs. You have pissed him off Sarah.'

'But mum.'

I started to talk, but she walked out of the room, closing my door behind her. I knew it was probably best just to go to bed like she had said but there was no way I was going to go straight to sleep.
It wasn't even six o clock in the evening, and I wasn't tired at all. I got myself undressed and climbed into bed, pulling my covers up to my head and placing my duvet cover in between my legs.
I always slept like that, in a ball on my side, like I was protecting myself while I was asleep.

The next morning, I woke up to the sound of the hoover on the landing, this was normal. Most morning's dad would have woken the whole house up with his cleaning. I am sure mum was happy to walk downstairs every morning to a spotless kitchen.
The radio was always on low because dad couldn't cope with silence, he used to say that the voices got inside his head if it was too quiet.
I opened my curtains, and the sun was shining brightly into my bedroom, just then my dad stormed into my room.

He marched towards me, slapping me full force across the back of the head, the slap was so hard I had to stop my head from hitting the glass window. He pushed me to one side and ripped the curtains closed again.

'They will see if you open them. And when they come it is all over for all of us. Do you hear me?' he scowled 'do you fucking hear me?'

I nodded my head, but I had no idea what he was babbling on about, I was starting to get used to dad talking in riddles and even more so since he returned home from Hollywell hospital.

'Get dressed and fuck off to school' he said,

'What about my breakfast' I asked.

'You can fucking starve for all I care, love. Why should I fucking feed a poisonous bitch like you?' he snapped. 'It's all your fault y'know, your fucking fault. Remember that when the shit truly hits the fan, now get dressed and get the fuck out of my house.'

It was just past seven in the morning when dad had pushed me out of the door, far too early to walk the ten minutes to school.
So, I knocked on my granny's door knowing she would be awake.
Granny was surprised to see me but I told her dad had kicked me out, she ushered me into the kitchen.

I had explained that I wasn't allowed breakfast that morning, so she made me some porridge and toast and started the whole conversation about how breakfast was the most important meal of the day.

She went on to tell me how disgusted she was with my dad for depriving me of food and said that no matter how naughty I had been it was no excuse.

While I was eating my porridge, there was a knock on the door. My heart started racing; I was sure it was my dad coming to tell me off, but I was proven wrong when my Auntie Amy had walked in. Granny started making a cup of tea and had offered me one too.

'Yes please,' I replied with a half-hearted smile on my face.

'What is she doing here' she said talking to my Granny

'One word – Jason' Granny replied.

Amy just shook her head and looked at me as if I was a piece of shit on her shoe; she then turned her back from me and faced the direction my Gran was in. She let out a big sigh and rubbed the palm of her hand across her forehead.

'You never guess what I overheard?' she said to my Gran.

Granny just looked at her and shook her head to show she had no idea.
'One of the art teachers at Saint Dominic's has been selling wacky backy to the kids, can you believe it?' she said concurringly.

'That's awful' Granny replied,

'Probably best not to talk about it now' she said pointing in my direction.

Soon enough it was time for me to go, I had met up with Stacey, and we headed towards school.

On the way, I had told her what I had overheard, and she was excited at the thought of a teacher selling drugs, she made light of the situation, and we giggled to each other most of the way.

We were by the cinema when Dylan had caught up; he had noticed us in front of him and sprinted down to catch up, so we waited. When he finally caught up, he was clearly out of breath.

He stood with his hands on his knees panting.

Stacey told him he was unfit for a little boy and he shook his head and smiled with the half grin he always did, still with one hand on his knee and the other hand on my shoulder, he had asked what the craic is.

'Sarah said our art teacher is a drug dealer' Stacey said with a big smile on her face.

'That is ridiculous' Dylan was looking at me.

'Hey, I just said what I overheard my Auntie saying to my Granny this morning' I replied defending myself.

'Well, I wouldn't let Mrs. Boorman or Mrs. Myers hear you say that' he replied.

I had to agree, and Dylan stood upright, patting me on the shoulder before we carried on our few minute walk towards the school. I hadn't thought about that conversation and just put it to the back of my mind, well that was until I was in art at the end of the week.

Our classrooms were big with colorful painting on the walls, and the two classrooms were joined by a small art studio in between. Some of the girls in my class including me were in the adjoining studio doing a big project that would be up on display in the corridor by the school's reception.

The day was going well, and the other two girls who were working on the project and I seemed proud that we were on target to finish the big five-foot masterpiece before the end of the lesson.

Then I heard Mrs. Boorman talking to some of the pupils in the classroom. A small freckly boy called Sammy McCoy put his hand up, I could see him from where I was working in the studio, our teacher asked what he wanted, and as the words came out of his mouth, I froze and dropped my paintbrush.

'Miss Can I have a five-deal please?' he said,

'What did you say' she asked shocked at the words coming out of his cheeky mouth.

'Sarah said you sell drugs miss, can I have a five-deal please?' Sammy was laughing so hard he almost fell off his chair.

Then the whole classroom roared with laughter, and Mrs. Boorman screamed for them to quieten down. Once the class had shut up, the silence was eerie, and you could hear a pin drop. I heard something slam down on the table and then the footsteps coming closer towards the studio room.
Mrs. Bormann walked straight past the other girls and me and walked through the door which joined the classrooms together. She returned a few minutes later with Mrs. Myers in tow, both looked red-faced and angry.

The other girls were asked to leave the room, but I was ordered to stay, my heart was beating fast, and I could feel my hands trebling in my blazer pockets.

Mrs. Myers closed both the doors to the joining classrooms and I was told to sit down, they both started telling me off and said to me that the police were going to be called as I was slandering a teacher. I tried to explain that I told one person a story I have overheard but they didn't listen to me. I was crying, and Mrs. Boorman just kept shouting at me. Eventually, I was asked to stand outside; I was told to walk through the classroom and wait in the corridor.

As I walked from the room through my class I kept my head down and paced as fast as I could, but I could still feel everyone looking at me, and I could still hear the sniggering from Sammy's big gob.
After about a ten-minute wait Mrs. Boorman finally came out into the corridor. 'You can go and sit by the office until the end of class' she snapped.
It was almost the end of the school day anyway, and I was just glad to get away from everyone for a bit, and the next day was the weekend. I was hoping it would have all blown over by then anyway, all these thoughts were going around my little brain, and then the realization of the situation hit me.

'Your parents have been called' Mrs. Boorman said as we got to the office, she pointed to the chair as if to tell me to sit and then she walked away.

As I sat waiting I could feel the tears building up in my eyes I knew that when I got home I would be in deep shit with my dad and that scared me more than the thought of the police getting involved.
At least the police could only tell me off, but my dad would kick all sense out of me, and I knew it, I fought so hard to stop the tears from escaping from my eyes, but it seemed the more I tried, the less chance I had. My head was starting to hurt, my bottom lip was shaking and the tears were forming puddles in the palm of my hand.

I was angry that I was crying, frustrated but overall scared of what would be waiting for me when I got home. It felt like I had been sat waiting for hours, but it was only forty-five minutes before the bell for the end of the day went off, I was just about to get up when Birdy called me into his office. Mr. Fulton was his real name, but we all knew him as Birdy. I walked into his room, and he closed the door and told me to take a seat.

'Sarah do you understand why you are here' he asked.

'Yes, but it wasn't my fault' I tried to explain

'Then whose fault, is it?' he asked looking at me over the top of the paperwork he was holding.

Shaking his head at me and he repeated the question. I couldn't give a reply because it was my fault; it was me and my big mouth that had caused this.
Birdy explained that I would be expelled from school and that my parents had been informed of the incident. With that I started to cry again, I knew for a fact that my dad would beat me when I got home for bringing shame on his family, so I tried to put it to the back of my mind and as Mr. Fulton was continuing to tell me how serious the accusation was.

I couldn't quiet hear what he was staying, my thoughts and fears of going home were at the forefront of my mind. I could see his lips moving, but I wasn't taking in anything he was saying. Then he said I could go home; I didn't hear him say it the first time, so he repeated himself louder and pointed to the door. I looked up at the clock and notice we had been in the office for almost an hour, so I knew I would be in the shit when I got home.

I got home over an hour later than usual, and my mum was out with Matthew.

Dad was waiting in the living room, and he had ordered me upstairs to my room, he was screaming and shouting so much that I couldn't understand half the abuse that was leaving his lips. I just remember being called a 'stupid slag' and a 'bitch.'
He walked out of the room and returned with a slipper in one hand and a leather belt in the other.

'This is going to hurt' he warned with a menacing smile on his face.

I coward myself into the corner of my bed, my back was up against the wall, and I was holding onto my knees, up against my chest to protect my body.
He swung the slipper first and got even more irate that he had missed me, so he grabbed hold of my hair, twisting it around his fingers and pulled me, so I was face down on my bed. He swung again, but this time I felt the hot stinging pain as the hard sole of the slipper connected with the bare skin on the top of my legs.

'That was meant to hit your arse you stupid bitch.'

He swung the slipper in the air again, and I tried to move out of the way, but that just added fuel to the fire, he was repeatedly hitting me with the slipper and eventually he stopped and asked why I wasn't crying.

'You can't hurt me anymore' I replied defiantly.

'Want to bet' he replied.

With that he threw the slipper on the ground, he still had the belt in his other hand, but by the time I noticed the slipper being thrown down, I felt such a pain in my back.

My Life in His Hands

I put my hands in the way as I seen his hands raise again above me and the belt came down again, this time it seemed harder, I screamed out in pain, and he was laughing at me.

'Stop fucking moving, or it will hurt even more' he warned.

I was begging for him to stop, but he just teased me by slapping the belt against itself to make a massive sound, then he swung at me again. The metal buckle smashed across my spine, causing me to scream out in pain, while he just laughed. I could feel the blood running down my back, and still, he continued to beat me with the belt. Then he stopped, looked down at me sobbing into a ball on my bed as if he was proud of his handy work.

He then turned and walked out of my room muttering something, but I was still sobbing so I couldn't make out what was said. I listened to his footsteps, and once I was sure he was back down the stairs, I got off my bed to attempt to clean the blood off my back. The cut was open, but not that deep. The blood kept coming out, and every time I wiped it, it would seep out again, so I grabbed the rope off my dressing gown and wrapped it around my body; covering the big gash in my back and tied it at the front of my stomach.
I was scared to make a noise, so I climbed into bed and lay there quietly until I finally fell asleep.

New School Again...

So, after the weekend spent in my bedroom for being expelled from Saint Dominic's, I was expected to get dressed in my school uniform and go back to the school. Birdy had rung our phone and demanded my parents bring me in at ten that morning. I was nervous enough as it was and then my dad started going on about how I was probably going to get arrested for slandering a teacher. I shrugged my shoulders as we walked out of our front door. Dad clipped me around the back of the head, and I almost lost my balance.

'You don't give a fuck, do you?' he snapped.

I didn't reply.

Once we were at the school, we went straight to the main reception and sat down to wait. My parents were called into Birdy's office, while I was asked to stay where I was seated. I was scared stiff and honestly believed that I was going to get arrested. But after twenty minutes, my parents emerged, and I was told to follow them.

Once outside, dad had started to let rip, about how I brought shame on their family, mum seemed upset too and explained that I would need to move schools. I was glad not to have to go back to Saint Dominic's but also sad.
I had made friends for a change, and I would have to be the new girl again, which I wasn't looking forward to.

'What school will I go to?' I asked.

'Whatever school will have you' mum had replied.

Then dad piped up 'you will stay at home if no fucking school will have you, you little bitch.'

It took two weeks, but I did get a new school, Saint Patrick's in Ballymena. It meant having to leave earlier and getting on a bus to travel to twenty-five minutes, change buses and travel another ten minutes. It sounded like a perfect school from what I had read on the welcome pack my mum had brought home with her.

'You are lucky I got you into that school' she said dropping the booklet onto the kitchen table and then walking to the far side of the kitchen.

She asked if I heard her, I nodded in acknowledge to what she had said and carried on reading.
Mum was still talking to me, but I was so engrossed in the text I was reading and didn't hear what she was saying, but I knew it was about the school I was due to start the following Monday.
Only four days to go I thought to myself.
Mum was pottering in the kitchen drawer for a pen and getting frustrated when she couldn't find one.
'Oh, for fuck sake Sarah, have you seen the pen?' she asked, I shook my head and closed the booklet in front of me.

'I will check in my school bag if you want.' I said as I got up from the chair.

My school bag was in my bedroom, so I walked up the stairs, on the second from last step was sitting one of slippers dad had used on me the week before.

I just froze and stood on the stairs, I knew I was stupid, and the best thing was just to ignore it, but this time I just stood there, staring at the slipper, knowing the pain it can cause, and I was shaking. Just then mum shouted into the hall to say she had a pen. I turned back around a walked down the stairs, I was so annoyed with myself that I had let the slipper get me down, so I shook the feeling off and ignored it, just like I did with everything else.

Ignoring the beating and abuse became normal.
I was grateful when dad was in a good mood, which wasn't that often. Mum needed the pen to sign some forms she required me to take with me on my first day of my new school.

The weekend flew by, and I spent most of the time out anyway, which kept me out of my father's way. I didn't want to go around to Claire's house with her perverted dad, so we planned to meet at the back of her house.

I was waiting for her for ages, but she didn't come out, so I walked over to Stacey's house.
She was out at the shop, but her mum had said I could wait inside, I declined her offer, thanked her and said I would wait outside as the weather was lovely for a change, so sat on the wall next to her house. Dylan must have noticed me from his window because he came outside and walked towards me with a big smile.

'What's happening?' he asked.

'Just waiting on Stacey.' I explained. 'She should be home soon; her mum said she is at the shops and on her way back.'

'Oh okay, I will keep you company until she gets here if you want?' Dylan said.

'I would love that' I replied with a smile.

We sat on the wall together holding hands, and I had gone into the whole story about being kicked out of school and starting Saint Patrick's the next day. Dylan seemed amused that I had been expelled.

'What's so funny about it?' I asked annoyed that he thought it was amusing.

Dylan just smiled and put his arm around me, as his arm brushed my back which still hurt from my beating and I flinch, I could tell he had noticed by the look in his eyes, but he didn't say anything.
He just released his squeeze a bit and placed his head on my shoulder.
'It will be strange not seeing you at school every day' he said looking up at me.

'I know what you mean, me and my big mouth eh?' I replied with a giggle.

Stacey had got home, and we all just sat chilling in the square, admiring the sunshine for a change. Elaina and Stacey were sat on the wall as Dylan, and I had walked over to his house, his mum had called him in for lunch, but after a mini argument with his mother, Dylan had finally got his way and had his dinner brought out for him.
So, we sat in the garden with our backs up against the wall, waiting. Dylan's little sister joined us; she was so cute, dark curly hair and a big smile always on her face. She had asked her big brother if I was his girlfriend.

'No, we are just friends' he told her.

That annoyed me, but I didn't let it show.

I just replied with 'best friends'

Sunday night I had gone to bed earlier than usual, I got everything ready for starting school the next morning and climbed into bed, I must have been asleep by seven that night.

The next morning, I was nervous as I was putting my new uniform on. I had assumed that I was traveling to school on my own.

Which was scary considering I had never been to Ballymena before and now I would be going there every day for school.

I was hoping I knew someone from Belfast and worried about making new friends. My worries were not needed as I got down the stairs, mum had explained she would be coming with me the first day. After my breakfast, I had got my coat on ready, and I was waiting in the kitchen for my mum when dad walked in.

'Have a good day, and try not to get expelled this time' he said,

'Leave her alone Jason' mum had replied.

I just looked down at the floor, wishing the ground would open and swallow me whole. I was relieved when mum said she was finally ready and we headed out the back door. I had to walk down to the bottom of stiles way, opposite Saint Dominic's school to catch my bus into Ballymena.

Mum was messing with hair, which I hated just as the bus turned up. I got on in front of her, and the bus was full of school-age children, but not one of them had the same uniform as me, and that made me feel uncomfortable. As my mum and I sat down on the bus, mum leaned over towards me.

'They are all prods on this bus for fuck sake.'

'I know, I will have to get on here on my own, tomorrow' I replied nervously.
'You'll be fine' she said, 'you sound English anyway, just keep your coat on' she giggled.

When we arrived at Ballymena bus station, we had to get on another bus to take us to my new school. The bus station was packed, but I felt a lot better when I could see other teenagers with the same uniform as me. Mum had told me to wait by the wall while she double checked what bus we had to get on. When she returned, she pointed in front of me, and we walked towards the bus we needed. I sat at the back of the bus because I hated feeling like people were looking at me, at least at the far end of the bus no one would be able to, not without me noticing.
Arriving outside Saint Patrick's College, the nerves kicked in.
Mum was lovely though and made me feel at ease.

'What if no one likes me?' I asked concerning

'Don't be silly' she replied, 'You are my daughter, so they have no reason not to like you' she smiled and walked towards the wall surrounding the school.

Once inside the school, it was like a maze to try and find the school reception.

'Think we came in the wrong way' mum said,

'I just followed you' I said with a nervous laugh.

We finally found the reception and were asked to wait in the corridor for the classes to get settled.
A teacher had walked past and asked if I was new, she explained that she was the music teacher and that she would see me around during the day.

'I hope you settle in well Sarah; I am sure you will.'
She said, 'I am Miss Hanna by the way, see you later.'

Mum was called into the office, and I followed her. She had already warned me that the staff needed to know why I was moving school, so I was half expecting a telling off from the teachers, but they were all welcoming, and my reason for moving school wasn't mentioned.
I was given a form to sign with the school rules on it, and they explained that I was signed into a contract and that if I was ever to be sent to the office for disruptive behavior that it would be recorded on the back of the form. I agreed with everything the lady was saying to me, even though only half of what was said was sinking in. After the forms were signed and I had been given a school tie, I was taken by another member of staff to my new classroom.
When the door was opened, I was shitting myself; everyone was staring at me. I just wanted to sit down and bury my head, but I was asked to stand at the front of the classroom and introduce myself.

I hated every second of standing in front of everyone, and I think it showed. When the teacher finished embarrassing the life out of me, I was told to find a seat. As I sat down a tall girl with long dark hair smiled at me and introduced herself.

'Hi, my name is Danelle, and this is Lynda' she said pointing to the blonde girl sat beside her. 'We are all friendly enough here, you don't need to look so worried' she explained.

We spent most of the lesson chatting quietly until a girl walked in.

'You're in my seat' she snapped looking down at me.

'Oh, I am sorry' I said gathering my things.

'Catherine can you just find another seat please' said our teacher

'But miss why should I have to move?' She replied,

'Just sit down now, you are already late' the teacher snapped.

I felt so awkward that I had stolen this girl's seat but Danelle told me to not worry about it, she explained that Catherine was funny with everyone but that she will be fine when she gets to know me.
I had hoped so, but she didn't give me much reason to believe them, every time I looked over in the direction where Catharine was sat, the looks I got from her was so undeserving. The lesson had gone quickly, and I was lucky to be in Danelle's class in my next lesson. We spent most of the day together, and both girls took me under their wing.

They made me feel welcome, and I was feeling positive by the time the end of the day came. I met up with Danelle at the end of the day, and she told me she and the girls were walking into town to catch the bus home, so she asked if I wanted to tag along with them. I can honestly say that I loved that school and I liked the fact that I felt far enough away from home, I could pretend that I had the perfect family life, when in real life it was anything but perfect. Once we had got into town, I headed straight to the bus station to head home, but I was happy that my first day had gone so well.

A Bit of Peace and Quiet...

My new school was the best thing that had happened to me in a long time. The only negative was that I seemed to lose touch with some of my friends in Saint Dominic's, but I gained some good friends in Ballymena. I started to hang around with Elaina a lot more often, and she would walk down to the bus stop with me most mornings.

Even though my school bus was full of pupils from protestant schools. I had managed to make friends with a girl called Laura.

The three of us would sit at the back of the bus most days talking about music and boys. Laura got off the bus before us; her school was on the bus route which was handy. Her school uniform was a bit to be desired though; her blazer was dark grey with a red trim and a big logo on the breast pocket saying Bailee High. I remember one day I was sat at the back with Laura and we were talking about boys, she had asked me if I had ever loved anyone.
I thought that was a silly question as I was almost thirteen and love seemed so far away.

'How can you love someone at our age' I asked.

She looked at me with a big cheesy grin and replied 'easy'

I looked at her and raised my eyebrow. 'I don't think I will ever love someone.'

Laura looked at me a little confused and said, 'bet you love your daddy?' I just laughed.

'Bet I don't.'

I went on to explain that they say if you can't trust your dad you can never trust any boys.

'And trust me I can't stand my dad' I said.

She didn't push the conversation and carried on talking about boys, she was in a relationship with a cute ginger-haired boy named Bobby. So, to her she felt like she was in love, they had been dating over a year, so it was no surprise that she was smitten with him.

'What about the lad you are with. What's his name again?' She asked.

'Dylan, Dylan Rhodes.' I smiled 'He lives by me.'

'That's so sweet, how long have you two been together now?' she asked.

'Err, just under a year now, but I don't see him much lately.' I started saying; then the lady sat in front of us turned around and looked at us both.

'Did you say Dylan Rhodes?' she asked,

'Yes, she did' piped up Laura 'why do you ask?'

The lady in front of us went on to explain that she was Dylan's Aunt Margret and that she had overheard us talking, I felt so embarrassed.

My Life in His Hands

I hadn't met Margret before but heard Dylan mention her, and I knew she worked in Ballymena, but I never expected to see her on the bus or anything. I remember thinking to myself that I was lucky I had only lovely things to say about him, whereas some boys I knew I could easily have bitched about them all day long.

Take Matthew Springer, for example, he was horrible to me, and we couldn't stand each other, even though my friends had said he liked me, he made a point of always teasing me which I had enough of at home, I didn't appreciate it when I was out with my mates as well. One day I was out on my bike when Matthew started chasing me with a stick.
He was trying to hit me, but I just rode my bike as fast as I could to get away from him.

I wasn't looking where I was going and ended up banging into a small foot tall big pile of breeze blocks. I flew over my handlebars, smashing my face off the curb in the process.

The pain so unbearable and I was screaming.
I could see the blood all over the curb, and I felt it gushing out of my nose onto the floor.
Matthew had run off at this point, and then I heard Jenny ask if I was okay. I looked up at her with blood all over me; I must have looked bad cause her little sister Lauren had run off to get help.
Jenny helped me to my feet, but I was dizzy and almost fell back down again, so I sat on the bloodied curb.

'Don't move a minute; I will go and get my mum.'
She said.

I wasn't planning to move anyway, the pain in my face was so sore, but the more I cried, the worse the pain was, so I tried to be calm and waited as Jenny had asked.

Lauren had already gone to get her mum, so the three of them returned to help me back to my feet. Lauren pushed my bike while Jenny and her Mum helped me to their house. The girls mum was a nurse of some sorts, so she had tried her best to clean my face up.

'I think you might need a stitch in that eye' she warned 'And I think you might have broken your nose'.

I never went to the hospital to get stitched up.
I had left Jenny's house and walked the three doors up to my own house and knocked on the front door with my bloodied hand. The walking had made the blood seep from my eyebrow and chin again. Mum opened the door to me and looked at me with horror, she then told me to hurry up in the kitchen and make sure I didn't get blood on dad's new carpet. My Auntie Pat was called to help clean my face up.

Dad had said that I wasn't allowed to go to hospital just incase the staff thought he had done this to me. I remember wishing I could have spoken but I had so many cotton wool balls placed into my mouth at the time I could. We both knew my dad would have never beaten my face. He was too clever to ever leave marks where they could be seen.

So, I had a lot of reason to hate Matthew, and he knew it.

After returning home from school the day I had seen Dylan's Aunt on the bus, I wanted to call for him and had arranged in my head to mine and eat my dinner as quickly as I could, so I could catch him before he headed out.

When I got home, the curtains were still drawn to a close, and mum was stood outside the front of the house, having a smoke and talking to Bernie; she was our next-door neighbor.
A lovely elderly lady who had so much love to give.
I had never seen any grandchildren go to her, so she took my younger brothers and me in and treated us like her own.

'What's up?' I asked my mum walking towards our front garden.

'Your dad is in Holywell again' she said looking lost and sad.

I must have smirked or something because Bernie gave me such a dirty look and told me I need to be supporting my mum. She said that I was horrible even to think my dad being in the hospital was a laughing matter, but she had no idea.
Hearing that my dad wasn't at home was fantastic news to me. I felt like a massive weight had been lifted off my shoulders and I could just relax and feel safe in my own home for a change.
I went straight upstairs to get changed out of my uniform, and I had no homework to do that evening as I had done it at lunchtime just to give me extra time out with Dylan and the gang.

I was still upstairs when I heard mum come back in and close the door. She shouted me to come down the stairs, and I told her I would be down in a minute, but she demanded I get down the stairs straight away. So, I did what I was told.

Stood only half dressed in the middle of the staircase mum started shouting, that I couldn't have made it more evident that I was glad my dad wasn't there, even if I had tried. She wasn't stupid and knew why I was happier knowing he wasn't in the house, and I think deep down she was happy too.

Even though she couldn't admit it, I knew she was grateful for some peace, just like me. I finished getting dress and told my mum I was off out, and I would be out the back of our house if she needed me, I told her about Dylan's Auntie on the bus and said I needed to go and see him, but she told me I needed to stay at home.

'I need you to watch the boys for me, while I pop to your Gran's and tell her what's happened' she said,

'Can you be quick?' I asked, but she just shook her head and walked out of the front door.

I didn't get to see Dylan for over a week and I had given up on the idea, and it seemed like mum would leave the boys with me at every given opportunity.

So as the weeks went on, I spent most of my time telling my naughty younger brothers off and cleaning the house. Mum cleaned don't get me wrong, but not as dad did. He was so paranoid about dirt and mess that he went over the top in his cleaning, and this was something I had got used to over the years, so I found myself cleaning up after my mum. On the odd occasion, I had annoyed my mother, and she snapped.

'You are worse than your fucking dad' she shouted 'always fucking cleaning after me. You know what do it your fucking self. Why should I even bother.'

I didn't mean to piss her off; I honestly thought I was helpful, and I didn't think I deserved to be tarred with the same brush as him.

In my eyes, he was a monster. So, to even get told I was acting like him or looked like him or anything made my blood boil. She had hurt me more saying I was like him than if she had beaten me with the spoon. The beatings were acceptable now.

My body had been used to the pain. The emotional damage was a whole different story altogether.
'Sticks and stones may break my bones, but names can last a lifetime' was my saying and remember that going through my head repeatedly for most of that afternoon.

So, thirteen days later I was finally allowed out, and the first thing I was done was knock on for Dylan. But he was away on holiday, and I had been told he was not due back till later that week.

With a heavy heart, I called for Jenny, and she was already out in the square at the back of my Granny's, so I went to meet her. She was at the local pot dealer's gaff, and the front door was always open. Even though she was younger than me, she had a seventeen-year-old boyfriend who would provide her with free smoke as a when she wanted it, in return for sex.

I had told her my concerns on many occasions, but she wasn't the type of girl to take advice, she would just shrug off any concerns.

When I walked into Guiney's flat, I noticed a very strong smell of cannabis and lager. The smell turned my stomach. Jenny was in the living room but looked off her face.

'Hey Sarah' she said all happy and jolly. 'Yo Mick, this is my friend I was telling you about. Isn't she sweet?' she said looking over at a big hairy fully-grown man, slouched on the floor of Guiney's pad.

'Very nice' the horrible sleazy man replied.

Shivers ran down my spine as he lay there staring up at me, his beard all messy and overgrown almost hid his yellow teeth and but I could still smell his stale breath from the other side of the room.
I felt sick to my stomach.

'How old are you wee one?' he asked, but I didn't reply
'Well don't you speak, or do you use your mouth for more important things if you get me?'

I knew what he meant, but I acted naively.

'No, I speak' I said, 'I am fourteen in July' I replied, July was over eight months away, but to me, it sounded better than being thirteen.

'Jenny tells me you like a smoke' he said snarling at me, his oversized nose twitching,

I looked over at her, and gave her a stare as if to say,

'Why would you tell him that.'

She looked nervous and just shrugged her shoulders at me.

'So, what if I do!'

He smiled and said, 'No don't take offense doll, I was just asking a question, no need to bite my head off.'

He then paused, looked down at his belt and looked back up at me 'I'm big Mick.'

I still felt uncomfortable and made my excuses to leave. I started to walk back towards the hall, and Mick stood up in front of me, to block my path.
He was big alright. He quite clearly got his name from his build. His shoulders were as broad as the door frame, and he was almost as tall as the door itself. There was no way I was getting past him.

'I need to go home.' I said, but he didn't move.
'Please my mum is expecting me, I need to go'

I looked over at Jenny for help, but she was so engrossed in sucking her boyfriend's tongue off that she didn't even notice me, and Mick stood at the doorway. Mick was looking down at me; he was playing with a big lump of solid in his hand, rolling it in his palm using his fingertips.

'You can stay for a wee smoke first' he said.

I went to speak, but he just put his finger up as if to silence me.

'That is the rules; you have to go by my rules. Do you understand?' he asked.

I just nodded my head, and he pointed to the two-seater sofa on the other end of the room.
I was a little scared, and I want to tell him to fuck off, but I didn't know how he would react, plus he was four times the size of me, so I did what I was told and sat on the sofa.

Mick started walking towards me and licked his lips, and then he moved the lump of solid towards his nose and gave it an extra-long false sniff. He sat down beside me, so I tried to move even closer to the edge of the sofa. Mick placed his hand on my leg. I tried to shake my knee as if the release his grip, but he just looked at me.

'That's better, now isn't it?' he asked.

'No, it's not!' I replied, lifting his massive hand from my leg.

He lends down beside the sofa to pick up a box, for a second I had a stupid thought that maybe he had a gun or something, but when he opened it, all that was in it was tobacco and cigarette papers.
He asked me if I could roll, but I told him I didn't smoke it.

'Don't lie, pretty face, Jenny wouldn't say it to me if it was untrue, she knows better than that' he said.

That afternoon I was forced to smoke and later forced to suck on Big Mick's penis before I could leave. I was crying and begging the bastard to leave me alone, but he grabbed me by the neck with both hands and threatened that he could break my neck, with one squeeze.

I was more scared of my dad than this man, but I knew if I didn't do what he said, he could have easily damaged me, his build against mine, I was clearly no match. It was apparent that I had no choice, so I did what he told me to. I was good at blocking out what was happening anyway. It was a skill I had learned over the six years of sexual abuse from my dad, so, I put my mind somewhere else. I just imagined I was on the beach having a peaceful stroll across the waterfront.

Every now and again my mind would bring me back again, but I tried my hardest to block out what was happening. In the end, I must have been rubbish, that or he realizes how fucked up it was getting a teenager to suck him off when he pushed my face away and told Jenny and me to get out of his house. He then threw what was left of the smoke in my direction.

'Enjoy your smoke, love. I hope it was worth it.'

I had been crying the whole time, but now as I looked at the smoke on the ground I was angry as if that sick bastard thought I did that to him for smoke, I did it because he scared the life out of me.

By throwing the smoke at me, he had made me feel like a cheap slag. A name my dad liked to use as well. Then I started to be angrier with myself than anything. I ran home not even saying goodbye to Jenny; I was so pissed off that she completely ignored what had just happened as if it was okay. It was far from okay, but with it happening so often I told myself that night, that I just needed to get used to it. That all men were the same and that it was normal. By normalizing it, I was making it easier to cope with in my young teenage mind.

Once home I retreated straight to my bedroom, I spent the whole night up there only popping downstairs to grab a bite to eat and even then, I took my sandwich back into my bedroom with me.
I had a small bedroom with only a bed and a tall wardrobe in it. I had a small cassette player on my window, which most of the time ruined my tapes by chewing them up.

It would be a mission trying to unravel the tape from the inside of the deck and most of the time I couldn't salvage whatever tape had been chewed up.

So, I started just listening to the radio. That became my sanctuary, and I soon realized I was safer in my bedroom now that the monster I called my dad was locked away in a mental hospital.

Big Mick had proved that I wasn't safe in my estate. With my dad abusing me, Claire's dad pinning me down and attempting to do shit to me and then Big Mick had forced me to do oral sex on him. I had convinced myself that it was all my fault. Maybe this is what I was meant to do; I started thinking. Why would all these people do these things if it wasn't my fault? I hated the fact that I was pretty, and I hated the fact that I was too scared to do anything about it. So, in my eyes, I was letting this happen to me, and I was thoroughly deserving of it for being a cheap slag. I know now that it wasn't my fault but as a thirteen-year-old petite young girl.
It was all because of me, and being pretty made it a whole lot worse.

I had been in my room for most of the afternoon, late on into the evening, when my mum walked into my room. 'What is up with you?' she asked, the look of concern on her face was a look I had gotten used to over the years, she sat down beside me on my bed and repeated the question.

'What is wrong with you, you have been locked up here all day, has something happened?' she asked,

'No, I am fine, I just want to chill on my own' I told her.

I wanted to scream at her and tell her I wished I was dead and that men love to hurt me, but what use would that have been, all I would have succeeded in doing was upsetting her, and taking my anger out on her. I couldn't bring myself to be horrible; after all, it was my fault, not my mums.

She had no idea what went on inside my head, and that's how I wanted to keep it. She got up from my bed and looked at me with a grin on her face.

'Well suit yourself' she said as she walked out of my bedroom, pulling the door to as she left.

I could tell she wanted me to open up, but what was the point, I have never been believed anyway. So, I decided to never talk about it again.

I had hoped that life would change and maybe my dad would be kept at Holywell, but even if he did. I remember thinking that it would stop the abuse because the two other men could still do the same to me.

Maybe it was a man thing; perhaps it was just me. Either way, I was safer in my bedroom than anywhere else. I had decided that that's where I would spend most of my time.

As the weeks went on, I maintained the belief that it was easier to hide away from everyone, than to let myself be put into another situation where I had no control over. I was good at understanding my mind and good at blocking out what was going on during all the abuse, but in my room with only my thoughts to occupy me, I had started to over analyses everything. I had come to the point that I was blaming myself for everything, and I was started to get scared of my own mind.

I had vivid images in my head about cutting my face and disfiguring myself so severely, that no man would want to abuse me. I had thought that it was my only option, but I knew I couldn't cause myself that level of pain.
That made me come up with a plan; if I couldn't disfigure myself, then maybe I could get someone else to, so I set out to make my plan work.

I knew full well that I couldn't just ask someone to do that to me, so I believed my best way to get it done was to go out and look for trouble, in the hope I would get a good kicking in return.

I was about to walk out the front door without telling my mum I was going out, but she saw me and called me into the kitchen. So, I stood in the doorway.
I was full of anger and rage because I had built up the courage to storm out of the house and get myself beat up.

That standing in the kitchen with my mother and little brothers made me think twice. 'How could I do that to them' I thought in my head.
Admittedly, I was selfish in my thinking.
If my plan had gone ahead, I would have been in a hospital, and my mum would have had to drag my little brothers to the hospital to come and see me.
I imagined the horror would have been too much, mainly for my brother's little young minds. So, I was back to square one.

'Sarah, Sarah! For fuck sake stop your daydreaming.
I was trying to talk to you, and you're not listening!' mum snapped

'I am' I replied defensively.

'What did I just say then?' she asked.

I had no idea what was said, and I just shrugged my shoulders, and she looked at me with such a disappointed expression on her face.

'Your boyfriend has been calling for you all day, and he says he needs to see you' she said,

'Who Dylan?' I asked

'Nah, stupid, who else? Well unless you are a tart with lots of boys.'

She said laughing. That comment made me sick in the stomach, but I pushed it to the back of my mind and told her I was going out.
I grabbed a packet of Walker's cheese and onion and went into the hall to grab my coat.
'Did Dylan say where he would be?' I asked, but she just shook her head.

I finally caught up with Dylan, and he seemed a little off with me, I thought it was because I had avoided not only him but everyone in almost three weeks. I felt guilty that I put myself first, but I was worried that if I asked him what was wrong, and then I might not like the answer, so I stayed quiet.

He was obviously acting weird with me when I went to hold his hand while we were walking around my estate. The Community Centre had a fun day on, so I had asked if we were heading there, but Dylan just stopped looked me in the eyes and said.

'Well I am, I don't care what you do'

I was shocked, he had never talked to me like that and I had a paranoid thought that maybe Jenny had said something.

After pulling him up on the way, he spoke to me he apologized and said that he just wanted us to be friends. When I asked why he couldn't give me a reason, just said that it wasn't working.

So, I told him I was going home. He didn't argue with me and said he would catch me later. I was angry and upset as I was walking toward the back of mine, just as I was about to cross the road I seen Keith.

He lived a few doors away from me and had asked what I was doing. I told him about Dylan, and he smiled at me, put his arm around my shoulder.

'It's his loss kiddo, look at you' he said, I just looked at him, and he smiled.

'You are a stunning pretty wee girl, and any boy who doesn't want to spend time with you is crazy, it is his loss. You remember that'.

He was right, I thought to myself, well for a moment and then I remembered how I had felt earlier on in the day. How I was going to get myself beat up so that I felt like I had some control over my life.
I hung around in my front square for just over an hour, Keith was playing his guitar, and I was in ore of him, but then I started to worry.

Maybe all boys will turn out to be classic monsters I thought to myself. All the men I had met so far, were monsters and they all wanted to hurt me.
With my mind racing yet again, I decided it was best to go back home and hide in my bedroom once again, so I made my excuses and left.

Once at home I went straight to my bedroom, slammed my door and fell on my bed in a big heap. I was crying uncontrollably, but not because Dylan had upset me.

I couldn't blame him for not liking me, after all, I hated myself, so could expect anyone else to feel any different towards me that what I felt about myself.

The emotions of the past four years had taken their toll on me, and it was the first time in over a year that I had cried as I did, I was sobbing like a wounded animal, and I was so angry with myself because of the situation I was still in.

Promising Changes...

So, it was the start of December, dad was still in hospital and life at home was starting to look up for me. At the age of fourteen, I was starting to regret the fact that all my friends had boys who they were smitten with, this seemed foreign to me. I couldn't quite understand when Elaina was always going on about this boy she liked. It was no surprise with the hell I had lived with, but it made me curious, I wondered if I could ever trust someone like she trusted her boyfriend.

She had tried on many occasions to try and set me up with a boy, but nothing ever came of it. One boy she never gave up on was a lad called Michael, he lived across the road from where we lived, and he played the guitar, he was kind enough, and good-looking, with mousy blonde hair and pale blue eyes, and I did fancy him.

Elaina would get frustrated with me and almost beg me to give him a chance, but her attempts failed. She must have thought I was weird because she would always bang on about how Michael and I were well suited, but I was having none of it no matter how hard she tried, I wouldn't budge.

Boys didn't interest me really; most teenage girls felt the need to have a boyfriend, the need to feel liked and the feeling of belonging to someone. Whereas I hated the thought of belonging to someone, my dad had made sure I felt like this anyway. Drumming it into my head, that boys were only ever after one thing. I wasn't prepared to take the chance. It was the only control I had in my life.

Christmas came and went; mum had spoilt us that year, with dad being away she wanted it to be as special as possible. I had a porcelain doll and porcelain masks for my bedroom wall and new stationary set that I had been asking for in the weeks leading up to Christmas.

Then after the twins and Matthew finished opening the last of their presents, mum walked into the kitchen, she called me in, so I got up, putting my new things on the sofa and went to see what she wanted.

'If I give you this, I don't want you to tell your dad, do you understand?' she asked.

I agreed and wondered what it might be as she passed me a rectangle present, wrapped in purple paper.

'What is it?' I asked,

'Open it, and you will see, but please just keep it to you.' I ripped off the wrapping paper, and I could feel my heart rate getting faster as I revealed a lovely book, made from leather with a peacock feather design embossed on the cover, it was perfect.

'It's a diary' mum said,

'After the last one you owned, I think it is best to keep it away, it has a combination lock on this one to make it harder for prying eyes, if you get what I mean?'.

I knew exactly what she was trying to say, I thanked her, gave her a big hug and ran upstairs to my room to put my new book away.

I figured that putting my new book under my mattress again wasn't the best idea as that was the place my dad found my last book, so I put it in the back of my wardrobe, under some clothes, I was confident it wouldn't be found in there.

When I returned downstairs, I asked my mum if I could go out for a bit and she asked if I could pop into my Granny's to drop some presents off with her, so I agreed and grabbed my coat. I should have known with it being Christmas day that most of my friends would out or busy, but I just wanted to be out of the house for a bit. I went to call for a girl called Emma.

She was a small dark-haired girl who always got bullied for being a bit trampy, but I knew you couldn't choose your parents or how they decided to look after us.
So, I could see past the un-brushed hair and off-white spice girl's top she seemed to live in. We had similar tastes in music most of the time, but I didn't like the spice girls really, but I also didn't have the heart to tell Emma I didn't like them, as she was so obsessed by the group. She was happy that I had called for her and we hung out in the square at the front of her house.
We were just chatting when a young lad walked past and smiled at me.

'He is a bit weird' she said.

'In what way?' I asked,

'I don't know, just seems a bit weird' she replied,

'Let's find out' I said with a big grin on my face.

Emma was begging me not to say anything, but I didn't listen, I just carried on walking towards his direction. The weird boy opened the gate to the house opposite Emma's, and I shouted,

'Hey you.'

He turned around and smiled again. 'What me?' he asked with a look of confusion on his face.

'Nah, the man stood beside you' I said in a very cocky tone.

He turned to look behind himself, and I burst out into laughter, by this point I was stood the other side of his fence.
Still giggling at him, he looked at me to ask what was so funny.

'You are, I can't believe you fell for it' I said still trying my hardest to compose myself.

'It's not every day a pretty girl talks to me with these big ears' he said raising his hands towards his head to wriggle his ears with them.

'Don't put yourself down, there are enough people in the world to do that for you' I said smiling back at him. 'I am Sarah by the way.'

He smiled 'Pleased to meet you Sarah, and I am Tommy, Thomas Strong' he said flexing his muscles.

Even though he wasn't a male model or anything, this boy made me laugh, and we stood talking for over twenty minutes. I looked around I seen that Emma had gone back in, so I told Tommy I was going to head back home.

'Well have a good day, oh and Merry Christmas' he said as I was walking away backward.

'And you Tommy, Merry Christmas.'

I must have had a big grin on my face when I got home because my mum had asked who had made me happy,

so, I told her about this apparently weird Tommy. She told me it was about time I had a boyfriend, but I dismissed what she was saying and nervously told her that I didn't know the first thing about him.

'Only one way to find out what he is like through' she said.

I listened to my mum's advice and decided I wanted to get to know Tommy a bit better, so over the holidays I had started to spend most of my time with him. He was thoughtful, and he was timid which I found endearing and sweet.
He liked me a lot, and I could tell he wanted to ask me out, but instead of putting him out of his misery and asking myself, I decided to act all cool.
I loved the slight control I had over him, this was all new to me, and I played on it a bit.

I knew within a matter of weeks, that if I asked him to do something for me, he would try his hardest to grant my wish, not in a wimpy, pushover way.
More in an 'I like you and want to make you happy way.'
That made me feel special, which was something I wasn't used to at all in my life.

I loved this new feeling of special, and it must have shown because my mum started picking up on it.

She would tease me and say I must be in love. That was
ridiculous as I had only known this boy for a matter of
weeks. Weeks, turned into months and Tommy and I had
started cuddling up to each other on his sofa, he was
always scared to make the first move, so I snuggled into
him tightly and moved onto his knee facing him.
I was playing with his hair, using my fingertips and gently
massaging his head; his hands were on my back stroking
me just as gentle. I was waiting for him to make a move
and when he didn't, I decided that if I wanted a kiss, then
I would have to make the first move. So, I placed my face
close to his, and I kissed him. You could tell he was
nervous, but he kissed me back, and it seemed to last ages.
When we finished, we looked at each other and giggled
nervously.

'So, does that mean you want to be my girlfriend' he
asked,

'What do you think' was my reply

'Well if I knew that, I wouldn't be asking' he said in a
cocky tone.

'I don't kiss any old boys y'know. Only special ones.'

So that was it, within eight weeks of being friends, we
finally became a couple and I spent most of my time with
him, I was finally starting to enjoy my life really, but I
always had the niggling feeling, that it couldn't last long.
As soon as dad was home, there was no way he would let
me have a boyfriend, after all, I was still a kid in his eyes.
Mum luckily was more down to earth and didn't mind,
well how could she have a problem with it, when it was
her idea in the first place.

To my mum, I was a young lady, but to my dad, I was still his little girl, one he loved to have complete control over, but never the less, and I was his little girl. So, I knew things would change once he got home from the looney bin.

My mum liked Tommy, which helped. He would often call around and chill in the living room, on a wet and windy evening with us, that was until dad got home, of course, me, mum and Tommy had agreed that is was best to not let on to him that I had a boyfriend. Mum said it was because my dad was overprotective, but I knew the real reason.

The day dad returned home I had told Tommy to stay away for a few days, he seemed to understand. I said that I would knock on for him when I could; he kissed me on the forehead and told me to take my time. Tommy had no idea about the abuse I had and was going through, and I had planned to keep it that way. I was worried that if he knew, he would treat me differently and that was the last thing I needed, he was my normal.

When I was with him, I didn't need to worry about anything else. At home, on the other hand, dad seemed just as messed up in the head as he was when he went into the hospital. I wasn't complaining though; I remember thinking to myself that at least we had been granted with a twelve-week break from him.

That evening I made my excuses to go out. I had told my dad that I was going to Claire's house and I had a feeling that he would have been stood at the back door and watched me, so I walked out my rear gate, straight over to her house and stood on her porch.

I didn't ring her bell I just stood there for a few minutes; I had guessed that my dad would have walked away from the back door after seeing me enter Claire's garden.

So, after the few minutes, I left the porch, I walked past the back of Stacey's house and continued down to the bottom of the estate where Tommy lived. When I got to his front door, someone was just leaving, I didn't know who they were, and I didn't take much notice, Tommy was stood waiting for me with a big smile. He pointed towards his living room, and I walked in, as I walked past him, he squeezed my bum, and I giggled nervously. The living room was dark and smoky, curtains drawn, and the television was on but down low. I sat down on the sofa and Tommy walked into the room with two glasses of juice.

'I hope you like Orange' he said,

'Thank you' I replied as he passed me my drink, he placed his on the floor and sat beside me.

'You fancy a smoke' he asked passing me a cigarette.

I reached out to grab it and asked if he had put weed in it, and he nodded and smiled at me.
We sat on the sofa for ages, Tommy was getting a bit more forward with me the more he smoked, his hands caressing my thigh, I didn't stop him even though I felt a little uncomfortable. I didn't want to make it obvious, so I leaned towards him and kissed him, as we were kissing his hand started getting higher, and higher, still kissing in muttered the words,

'What if we get caught?' Tommy didn't answer; he just slowly lowered his hand, back towards my knee

'Sorry' he said pulling away from me.

I spent over half an hour telling him that I would let him know when I was ready to go further with him. It worried me that if I didn't give into him soon, I might have lost him, at the same time, he feared that if he was too forward, he might scare me away. Tommy was older than me but only by two years, but it was his sixteen birthday, was a week later.

We had a conversation, which if we didn't do it soon, we would have to wait till I was sixteen.
Otherwise, he could have gotten into trouble with the police for sleeping with a minor.
I still wasn't ready, and I made sure he knew that, but Tommy is the caring, considerate human being, he understood, one hundred percent that this was a decision that he would have no control over.

Nothing Lasts Forever...

It was May 1998; dad hadn't abused me since he had come out of the hospital earlier that month, so I started to guess that maybe his trip to the hospital, had some effect on him after all. I was at school on a Tuesday afternoon, and I started to have a niggling feeling that something was wrong at home, I know it sounds silly, but I just had this gut instinct that something wasn't right, I was worried that maybe dad had turned on mum again. The last time he had, he put her in hospital. I went to the school office and told them that I didn't feel well. I had convinced myself that they would send me home early, but instead, I was told to sit in the nurse's room till I felt better.

When my home time finally arrived, I couldn't wait to get outside the school. I felt sick with worry, I had been overthinking and got myself, into a stupid state. I waited for the bus and didn't speak to anyone on the way home. Once my bus had got to the bus station in Ballymena, I realize the bus I needed to get me back to Belfast was about to leave.

I ran towards it, almost knocking a small girl down in the process. I felt terrible, but at the same time, I knew I had to be home as quick as I could. I ran up the Stiles road and straight to my house, and I was out of breath by the time I got to my back gate. I stopped to catch my breath and noticed that all the curtains were drawn again. Of course, I thought the worst and ran in through the back door. Dad was sat at the kitchen table tapping the table with his fingers, and mum was sat in the living room, in silence. I walked into the living room to ask mum what had happened, and she told me I was better off talking to my dad. I turned to look at my dad, and it was clear he had been crying.

'What wrong daddy?' I asked

'Come and sit down, Sarah, please. I need to talk to you.'

So, I sat down and got ready to listen to what he had to say. 'Do you know Granny has been ill lately?' he asked.

I explained that I knew she had been in the hospital for a minor operation, but that she was fine, and then I asked why I was being questioned.

'Your Granny… My mum…' he paused to compose himself. 'Granny is ill Sarah, and she has cancer, but it has spread' he burst into tears.

As sick as he made me feel, I could help but feel sorry for him. I didn't know what to say, as I watched this fully-grown man, sob like a small child, making long sighs in-between his deep, shaky breaths.
He reminded me of myself, the way my body would shake uncontrollably after he had finished abusing me.

That made me feel sick, so I walked into the living room, where my mum was still sat and told her that my dad needed her. I explained I didn't know what to do, so she got up and told me she would swap places with me.
I sat where my mum had been and guessed my mum had been sat on the sofa most of the day, as the couch was dented where her body had been.

My Life in His Hands

The seat was warm, I could hear my mum talking to my dad, but she was whispering so I couldn't make out what was being said.
The atmosphere was intense, so I made my excuses and went to my room to do my homework. About an hour later, mum had brought me some curry up for my dinner.

'I guess you want this up here?' she asked passing me my plate.

'Your Granny has got cancer love, and there is nothing the doctors can do for her' she said in an upset tone.
'Everyone has known for weeks, but we only got told now, because of how ill she has got' she continued.

'Why did we only get told now?' I asked annoyed that we were always last to know like we were the outsiders in the family.

'No one wanted to say anything to us because your dad has not long been out of hospital again' was my mum's answer.

That made me angrier, 'Oh poor Jason' I snapped.
'I will ignore that comment' she said as she walked back out of my bedroom.

I ate my dinner and decided to have an early night, I had told Tommy I would meet him, but I didn't feel in the mood to see anyone. I just wanted to crawl into bed and fall asleep. The day had been terrible; I had done my homework so didn't see any reason to prolong my day. As I got undressed I heard my mum putting the boys to bed, I stood on the other side of my bedroom door, waiting for her to finish and go back down the stairs.

Once I heard her, I went to the bathroom for my wash and stared in the mirror for a while. I started to think about my Granny really, and the emotions came flooding out, I was crying my heart out, but this point I was sat on the bathroom floor, but my tears were silent, that didn't take any of the emotion away if anything it would intensify the trauma I was feeling. Not being able to release the sounds when I cried made the feelings hurt deep in my stomach muscles. I am not sure how long I was in the bathroom, but I was interrupted when the door knocked, so I composed myself, stood up and threw water over my face.

The door knocked again, so I opened it. It was Callum, as soon as I opened the door, he started bitching at me, so I pushed past him and stormed into my room, closing my door behind me.

My room was dark, but I just sat behind my door for a while and let my mind wander. I was good at pretending I was some mage or witch, and I had read about astral projection. I had convinced myself that I could take myself away from my life every now and again to compose myself and arrange my thoughts more clearly, I knew this sounded strange, but it was my way of coping at the time.

The next day I was sent to school as normal, I was quiet, and not really in the mood to talk to anyone. I had seen Danelle as soon as I got off the bus, and I told her about my Gran, she understood and said to me that everything would be okay and if I wanted to talk she would be there waiting with tissue. I told her I was fine, but throughout the day she would come over to me and tell me that sometimes it was good to talk. She knew I wasn't fine, even if I was trying to convince myself that I was.

My Life in His Hands

That evening the whole family went to my Gran's house,
everyone was there, even my dad's ex-wife Sandra was
downstairs in the kitchen, and she had brought Connor
and Shane.

As I walked up the stairs, I could hear people in my
Granny's bedroom. I looked in the room, and I see my
Granny, asleep in her bed.
She had lost so much weight, and she had bruises all over
her arms, I had guessed those injuries were all over her
body as well. Everyone was crying, and I know it was sad,
but I couldn't cry in front of anyone, I didn't want my last
memory to be sad, so I pushed past my Uncle Paul and sat
on the bed beside my Gran.

She opened her eyes and looked at me. As weak as she
was she reached out her hand to grab mine, I smiled at her
and told her I love her, she smiled back. I lent down
towards her to kiss her on the forehead

'I know' she said.

I looked at her confused, and she mouthed the words

'I know your dad and you.'

Tears were building in my eyes, and I whispered, 'it
doesn't matter' in her ear.

She then patted my hand and whispered, 'Sorry.'

I looked at her as tears fell on, both of our cheeks. I
wondered how she knew, but that was enough for me.
At least someone was finally on my side and believed me.

The next day I couldn't stop thinking about what my Gran had said to me, I kept repeating it over and over in my head.

I wanted to tell someone, but I knew I couldn't. I was going crazy inside my head, I had so many unanswered questions, like how long had she known? And how did she know? Maybe as a mum you kind of sense these things, maybe she knew more about him than she let on, or maybe there was a slim chance that my dad had told his mum and that's why she forced him to go into Holywell. It was early afternoon on Thursday 14th May; I was in the canteen at school eating my lunch, when my form tutor Mrs. McQuillan walked up to me, she sat on the table beside me and told me that I need to go home after my lunch.

I knew why straight away, and I couldn't eat anymore, so I pushed my tray away from me, my teacher asked if I was okay and if I wanted a lift home, but I declined and told her I had a bus ticket anyway. She walked me down to the bus stop once I grabbed my things, and told me that it was my Granny and that my mum said I would know what the phone call meant.
I looked at her and nodded my head, you could see she felt uncomfortable, so I told her I was okay, and she didn't need to stand with me. After a few awkward seconds of her staring at me, she finally left me in peace.

The bus journey home seemed to take a lot longer than normal, when I finally got home, the front door was locked, which meant both my mum and dad were out. I walked down to Amy's house, and no one was in there at all, just the dogs barking like mad.

So, I decided the only other place was my Gran's, I was convinced that this was bad in my head, and by the time I got two doors away at my Gran's house, I could see through the kitchen window that everyone was in the house.

I walked into the house and went straight up the stairs towards her bedroom, she looked even skinnier, and the bruising on her arms were even darker, the tears rolled down my face, and I just stood there staring at her.

I looked towards the door because I see someone in the corner of my eye, I hadn't seen this man before, he was a priest who had come to give my dying Granny her last rights, I was too much for me, and I rushed out of her bedroom towards the bathroom. My mum was in there, sat on the bath, crying her heart out, I put my arms around her and held her as she sobbed on my shoulder.

That evening, the twins and I were sent up to my Uncle Ron's house in North Belfast. I remember thinking how posh his old Victorian house was compared to our council house, tall ceilings and picture rails, it was terrific.

I could ignore the fact that everything was stressful back home and imagine I was millions of miles away. That night I slept like a baby, I was asleep by nine o clock that night and slept through till nine the next morning.

I woke up and for a second forgot that my granny was dying, then I felt guilty that I did almost forget. The questions I had when she confessed she knew still went around in my head.

I knew I couldn't ask her what she meant, and she wouldn't have been able to tell me, her health and appearance have disintegrated so much in twenty-four hours that I knew the next time I saw her, she would be even frailer.

Ronald and his wife took me and the twins to the park before we headed back home. While at the park I had found a soggy five-pound note in between the bark of the playground.

I remember being excited.

We got into the car after spending a good hour at the park. I had told the twins that I would buy them something from the 50p shop in town, so they were happy. When we got to my gran's the house it was silent. Something clearly wasn't right, and you could feel it in the air, the hairs on my arms and back of my neck stood on end, and a shiver took hold of my body. I walked into the kitchen with the twins, and my mum was sat at the kitchen table, with my Auntie Pat.

'Sit down please love' she said to me, so I did what she said and pulled out a chair from under Gran's table.

Stupidly I asked her what was wrong, but I could tell by the look on everyone's faces.

'Granny died a few hours ago love, peacefully in her sleep' she said.

The day went by, and I was in a weird state of calm, even when the undertakers returned with Granny's body I was still okay. Everyone in Gran's was in floods of tears, but I couldn't cry. I wanted to so everyone didn't think I was cold hearted, but the tears wouldn't come.
I walked from room to room in a daze and then I went into the living room where my Gran's body lay in the open coffin. I sat on the sofa, with paper and coloring pens I had in my school bag and started to write a poem.
It was titled 'In loving memory,' and it was clearly a poem about my Gran.

Once I had finished writing, I folded up my poem and walked towards the coffin. Granny looked different, the undertakers had put makeup on her, and her face looked almost wax-like.

I went to stroke her head, but as soon as I touched her cold hard skin I freaked out, pulling my hand back towards me as if I was burnt or something, I stepped back to compose myself. The feel of her skin scared me, after all, I was a child still, and this was the first time I had ever seen a dead body, and this was the women who always loved me no matter what, she was the glue that held the family together, and now she was gone.

I walked back towards the coffin and placed my poem down the side of my Gran's arm. I then kissed her forehead and walked back out of the living room.

The next day I woke up early, as I got down the stairs mum was sat at the kitchen table.

'You missed it all this morning' she said,

'Why what happened?' I asked looking around for my dad.

'Where's dad?' I asked her

'Down at Amy's, there was a fire this morning in Granny's house, it started in the living room. Vee is suffering from shock because she woke up on the sofa, with the room in flames' she continued. 'Amy and your uncle Derek got the coffin out in time' she paused for a second, wiped the tear that fell from her eyes 'Granny's body is now at Amy's, and the funeral is on Monday.'

I was struggling to take it all in and wondered how on earth the fire started.

I was glad when I knew everyone was safe. I didn't go to Amy's over the weekend; I didn't see the need to put myself through seeing my deceased Gran all over again. The next time I would see the coffin was on the Monday of the funeral.

Even that Monday went past like a blur, and I honestly don't remember much about the funeral or the days that followed. I spent as much time as possible away from mine and my Gran's houses. I spent most of the day down at Tom's, smoking weed, which seemed to help, and Tommy and I was making plans for my birthday. He was good at taking my mind of stresses, and as harsh as it sounded at the time, I knew life had to go on, and my Gran lived a happy and full life. Tom and I were cuddling and kissing on the sofa, and for once in a long time, I felt safe again.

Growing Up...

It was the middle of July and Tommy, and I had been together for a year and a half, I had just celebrated my fifteenth birthday and Tom was sixteen at the time, we had started to have a lot of conversations about, when I was older we would lose our virginity together. We really believed that we were in love and that we would spend the rest of our lives together. We spent many days talking about our future, we planned our first time down to a tee, Candles, incense and soft music were all included in our plans, but even the best-made plans never work out. Our relationship had become more intermit, but we knew that we couldn't do anything about the passion building up inside, if we had given into our urges, Tom could have got into trouble. It was against them for us to sleep with each other as it was classed as sleeping with a minor, so we had decided to wait another year until we were both old enough.

'You are well worth the wait' Tom would tell me regularly

A few weeks later, on a beautiful summer's afternoon we had decided we couldn't wait any longer, well if I am honest, I was scared that if I didn't give in soon, Tom would start to look elsewhere, and I feared to lose him.

So, when it conversation came about again, I agreed that I was ready. I couldn't really say no when we had been experimenting a lot. Lately, it always got to that awkward moment when we would have to stop and just hold each other.

We were in Tom's bedroom, I was wearing a skirt and a thin strapped top, I was feeling slightly insecure, but Tom made me feel at ease. This was the moment I thought to myself as his hands started to rub the top of my leg, we were both lying down, kissing and caressing each other's body, his manhood was stood to attention, so I took it upon myself to do something to help. I slowly undid his buttons on his jeans and was just about to get his penis out to play with it, when his mum walked into the bedroom.

'Oh, shit sorry' she said covering her eyes. I was mortified and quickly sat up and fixed my skirt back into place.

Tom buttoned himself backed up and snapped at his mum, for just walking into his room.

'I pay the rent' she snapped back.

'Come on Sarah, let's go out' he said turning towards me.

I stood up and grabbed my jacket, not that it was needed, the sun was shining down, and for Northern Ireland, and it seemed like a heat wave.

We started walking out of our estate, hand in hand, down towards Saint Dominic's. I decided it would be a bright idea to climb over the fence to have some time on our own on the school grounds.
We were chilling at the bottom of the school, near the old airplane hangar, when we see the shed had been left ajar, so me being me, I had to investigate. Tom was worried that someone was inside, but I didn't care.

'Come on you chicken shit' I said mocking him

'I don't want us getting in trouble' he replied,

'I thought I was worth it?' I teased as I walked into the small stone shed.

He followed me eventually, and we stood inside, the place looked like it had been used as some ritualistic place. It was dark, but the walls were painted in bright primary colors. One of the paintings was a bit scary, it was a massive face with its mouth open, and it looked like spiders were coming out of the mouth, but because it was dark, it was hard to make out exactly what the painting was.

'Looks like we have found the perfect place not to get disturbed again.'

I said smiling at Tommy, he looked more nervous than me and pointed towards the dirty floor.

'I won't be lying on that' I said in disgust.
The floor was dirty, and I wasn't going to get my clothes dirty, but in this small shed was some school chairs stacked up in the corner of the room, so I picked up two chairs and put them together.

'That doesn't look comfortable' Tom said concerning.

I just shrugged my shoulders and walked towards him, sucking on my little finger, I could tell I was teasing him, and I loved the fact that I had complete control over the situation. As I got closer, I could see the nervous twitch at the corner of his mouth.
I placed my hand on his cheek and asked if he was sure that this was what he had wanted.

'Oh, I am sure. I just don't want you to feel rushed.' I smiled back at him still stroking his face with my hand, and I demanded he kisses me.

'It's not how we planned I know.' I said looking into his eyes 'but at least we are on our own for a change, and at least we are in control.'

We were passionate with each other, but very clumsy as well. First, I started by sucking his penis, which I had done a few times before, but this time was different.
I wasn't worried that it would go too far, so I was able to let go, and for a change I didn't think about my dad when I was doing it, I was more worried that when we did finally sleep together that I wouldn't know what to do.

I was good at oral, I knew that from the seven years of having to please that monster at home, but this was going to be the first time I had ever had sex.
I was scared and excited at the same time, and the nerves clearly showed on both sides. Tom had laid me down on the chairs, but the metal bars which interlinked the school chairs dug into my back, so Tommy put his jeans over the metal. He asked if that was better but even though it wasn't I agreed.

We struggled to start off with, so Tom used his fingers to try and ease my private parts open when he finally thrust himself inside me, I felt a ripping sensation, but it didn't really hurt, not as I expected anyway. The whole time we were making love, Tom was asking if I was okay and if it hurt.

I reassured him I was fine and eventually we had finished. My back was sore, and my legs felt all wobbly. I was giggling nervously, and Tom thought I was laughing at him, but once I had told him that it wasn't, he was fine with me.

We spent the next hour just staring at each other and giggling at what we had just done.

'Something to tell the grandkids' I joked

'What that we broke into your old school to lose our virginity' he laughed.

'You were perfect by the way' Tom said with a massive grin on his face

'And you weren't too bad yourself' I said, 'not bad for our first time eh?'.

We had returned home as Tom had work that evening, and needed to get back to get ready for his shift. We had agreed that we would meet up two days later as he was working the next day too, we kissed and said goodbye, and I headed off home.

Once I got home, my dad was still acting strange, the curtains were still closed, and the house was in darkness, even though it was a beautiful day outside. I didn't want to ask why so I just walked over to the sink in the kitchen, to pour myself a drink.

'Where have you been?' dad snapped

'Just out' I snapped back.

'I know you have been fucking out; I am not that stupid. I asked where the fuck have you been?' his voice getting louder.

'I was with Emma' I said.

That seem to stop the questions, but I knew he didn't believe me, I was worried mum had already told him about me having a boyfriend, and I was so scared that if he knew I was with someone, that he would punish me in a way that only he could.

Moving Yet Again...

It was the ninth of August, and I had arranged to stay out all night with Tommy, I had told my mum and dad that I was staying at Claire's house overnight, and my dad was okay with that. Being the ninth of August meant that there were bonfires arranged and marches for the Catholic parades. Just like the twelfth of July for the orange marches, August was our day to be proud and living in Ballymore we were almost guaranteed to have a good night.

I met up with Tom about seven o clock that evening, and the bonfire was just about to get lit. To start with I didn't see Tom at all and I walked around aimlessly until I finally noticed him. I was paranoid that my dad would see us, so we had arranged to go into town and chill with Tommy's mates for the evening. We were at a house party, and drinks were flowing, but I didn't remember most of the night, I just remember making up the next morning on the sofa, with Tom asleep in a sitting-up position at the bottom of me.
I kissed him on the forehead, and he smiled at me, his eyes still closed he mouthed the words 'I love you.'
We got ready and made our way back to our estate. I was worried just in case my dad had known that I stopped out, somewhere other than where I had said I would be.
I was even more apprehensive when I was walking up the road and seen Claire's brother and dad walking up the street.

'Hello love' shouted her dad

'Is she in?' I asked.

'No, she stayed out last night, we are only back now, but she isn't due back for a few hours' he dad explained.

That made me worry, even more, because what if my mum and dad knew that Claire had stayed out that night, I would sure be in the shit. I walked straight towards my back gate, and yet again all the curtains were drawn closed, for a change this filled me with relief as I guessed my dad had stayed away from the window which I was talking to Claire's family.

As soon as I walked through the back door, dad had started shouting at me.

'Close the fucking door' he shouted 'They will come and get me; do you want that? Do you want that?' he screamed in my face.

I knew better than to answer him back, but that seemed to feed the fire. He was still screaming in my face when I snapped back
'I don't know what you are talking about' with that he swung at me and missed the first time so started to swing his arms uncontrollably towards me.

I cowered into a ball by the back door, and he was hitting me in the head, repeatedly while he screamed at me that everyone knows.

'No one knows' I begged, but that didn't stop him.

Mum ran through the kitchen begging him to leave me alone, and saying that I had no idea what was going on, he stopped at looked down at me 'Sorry' he said and walked away. Mum came over to me and asked if I was okay.

'What did you say to start him off again' she asked

'Nothing' I replied, but from the look on her face, she didn't believe me.

I made my way past the living room where dad was sat, hoping that he wouldn't notice me, and I went straight up to my bedroom. I put my stereo on low and got my secret diary out to write about the past few months, I hadn't got it out since my dad was home from the hospital, through fear of him seeing it, but I was getting to the point that I didn't care anymore. What was the worst thing he could do to me, I was sure he had done his worst anyway?
It was a few days later when mum told me that we were moving away, I had said to her, that I didn't want to leave, but she just snapped and told me I had no choice in the matter.

I had asked when we were going because I needed to say goodbye to my friends, and she informed me I only had a few hours before we were leaving. I ran to my bedroom in floods of tears, how could they drag me away yet again? I thought about standing my ground and refusing to leave, but that wouldn't have solved anything. Mum walked into my room, but I just stood with my back towards her and listened to her try and reason with me.

'We have no choice love, we have to move' she said

'Why, why the hell do we have to move yet again?' I asked demanding an answer.

'It's your dad's choice, not mine' she said defending herself

'And why do you always listen to him, the way he treats us, and still you bow down to his every wish, I hate this shit, and I hate my life' I said storming past her and I headed straight out the front door.

I was angry and went to knock on Tom's house to tell him that I had to leave, the thought of running away was at the forefront of my mind, but I could only do it if Tommy agreed to come with me. I knocked on his door quite loudly and after a few seconds his mum answered.

'Hello love, Thomas is at work. I will tell him you called' she said,

'No point I will be gone by then' I said as I burst into tears on her doorstep.

His mum felt terrible and I could tell, she had offered me in to wait on him, but I explained that I was leaving in a few hours. I had written a note on a piece of paper that she handed me, and she promised that she would give it to him as soon as he was home. So, I left with a heavy heart and decided to knock on for Stacey, to tell her my sad news.
She was out the front of hers with her sister.

'Hey' she shouted over.

I didn't reply I just looked at her as I walked closer to the wall they were sat on.

'What's up with you?' Stacey asked as I got beside her

'My fucking dickhead of a dad has decided we are moving back to Crosby' I said with a shaky voice.

'What the hell, why?' she asked,

'God knows what goes on in his fucked-up head' I said lowering my head.

'When are you moving?' Stacey's sister asked.

I looked down at my watch and told her I had less than an hour before I needed to be back at home.

'That is so unfair' they both agreed.

My next stop was to Claire's house; she lived by Stacey anyway, so I only had a few feet to walk. I knocked on her door, but her mother informed me that she was out and wouldn't be back till later in the evening.

'I will be gone by then' I said as I walked away.

It seemed like no one was in, and I needed to say my goodbyes, but typical Jason, got what he wanted. Maybe I wasn't told beforehand, so I didn't have time to make plans, surely dad hated me enough to leave me behind and when I saw him a few minutes later. I had asked if I could stay with my Auntie Amy. My answer was one I should have expected really, he snapped.

'You are my fucking daughter, you belong to me, and you do what the fuck I tell you, do you understand you ungrateful little bitch, you belong to me and always will be.'

I stormed up into my bedroom, slamming my door shut, but it wasn't like my room anymore, the bedroom had been stripped of anything that belonged to me. So, I sat on my empty bed, and I cried and cried. I am sure my mum and dad could hear me, but I was ignored.

So that was it, we were set to leave everything I had known, behind yet again, all because my dad had said so, I should have been used to it, but leaving Tom was the hardest thing I could do. I wanted to run away, but I knew I had nowhere to go, and I knew I had no choice.
In the letter, I left with Tom's mum, and I had put in it that I would be back one day and that I understood if he got another girlfriend, but that I would be thinking about him and that I would return to Belfast as soon as I could.

Back Tracked...

So, it was mid-August 1999; we moved over in such a rush that we had nowhere to go apart from my Nan's house, nothing seemed to change in the years we had lived in Ireland, Crosby looked the same as it did when we left. We got out of the taxi outside Nan's and walked towards her front door; I was at the door first and just stood there waiting.

'Open the fucking door' dad shouted at me.

'I can't just walk in' I said as he walked faster towards me.

'Fucking move out of the way you dickhead' he snapped pushing past me to open my Nan's front door.

Once inside, I took our bags into the kitchen. It looked no different. Still, the same green wallpaper, the same furniture in the room, even the Murphy's Law tea towel still hung on the back of the door.
It seemed weird that nothing changed really because my life had changed so much. My abuse was happening more often, and I was getting older in so many ways, yet time seemed to stand still back in Crosby.

I was called into the living room where everyone was. When I walked in and seen Nan sat on her same armchair in the corner of the room, I walked over to hug her.

'Wow you have grown' she said. I just smiled at her

'You have got smaller Nan' I joked.

Just then a young man walked in the room behind us, Mum seemed to know who he was straight away and was greeting him with the usual lingo 'Long time, no see.'

I had no idea who he was and then Nan explained that he was my cousin. He was my Aunt Margret's son, and that he was living with her.

'Hi, I am Wayne' he said,

'I'm Sarah pleased to meet you' I said in a timid voice.

We all sat in the living room while mum made everyone a hot drink. Wayne was talking to me and the twins about music, but the boys didn't seem interested. Within a few minutes of talking he had told me how much he loved Michael Jackson. This was something we had in common, and he had told me I should see his room, so I agreed and followed him upstairs.
His place was covered in Jackson memorabilia. Bed covers on the wall like a big fabric poster.

Another poster from Michael's album covers filled up most of the wall space, and every bit of space was Michael Jackson something, his mugs, coasters, and even the pens. It seemed like everything was to do with the king of pop.

'I like Michael, but not as much as you' I said giggling.

'You have a cute laugh' was Wayne's only comment.

We settled into Nan's okay and I was asked what school I wanted to go to. Mum wanted me to go to Thomas Bracken.

It was a posh school, and you needed to do a test to get into the school, but I was smart and that didn't bother me really, dad, on the other hand, wanted me to go to Holy Trinity, it was the only Catholic school in the area, but after spending a while thinking about my options I asked if I could return to Saint Michael's.
Dad thought I was crazy about what to go back to that shite hole of a school, but because I was there before, I was adamant that that's where I wanted to go. After an hour-long debate, I finally got my way. I was looking forward to seeing my old friends, including Annabelle. So, mum sorted it all out for me eventually anyway; it seemed to take weeks to get me started.

I was in my last year and getting ready to do my GCSE's so I was keen to get back into a routine as soon as I could, but I had to wait, and wait. I finally started school, two weeks after everyone else had started.

In the weeks leading up to starting school, I had spent a lot of time with my new cousin. He was nine years older than me, but he seemed to enjoy my company, and we spent hours listening and debating, the king of pops tunes. We would watch the music videos and comment on how much it cost to record them. The video for Michael's single; Ghost for example cost over two million pounds to make, which seemed ridiculous just for a four-minute video. Wayne would teach me the dance moves and how to do the famous Moonwalk. So, when I got told it was near October before I was starting the Saint Michael's, I wasn't too miffed.

I was in my own world of Michael Jackson, so I didn't care really.

The next day I went to see my friend Matti, he was basically, a cousin to me, and we had known each other off and on since I was a baby. I remember sitting around his kitchen table and just catching up over the past few years. It was apparent to me that he liked me, but I used that to my advantage. I knew he would do almost anything for me, I had him make me cups of tea, and he even stole a cigarette off his mum to try and impress me. Matti's mum Gail didn't like me; I could tell by the way she looked at me, so I would egg Matti on when it was something that involved her.

Later that day I went to knock on for my old mate Tori, she wasn't in, but her older brother Alan answered the door.

'Hello stranger' he said.

I liked Alan when I was younger, and now he had matured into a good looking young man. I stood on the doorstep for ages flirting with him. I loved the attention, and with my past, I thought that was what men expected of me.

I felt guilty at the same time because it had only left Tommy in Ireland a few weeks before, but I had guessed he would have moved on anyway. I was young and single, and Alan didn't seem to mind.

I had agreed to meet up with him later in the week, and I did. We hit it off straight away, and before long, he was introducing me as his girlfriend.

We both loved Michael Jackson, so that helped.
The weekend before I was due to start school, I was with Matti and his mate, who was also called Allen, but with two L's in his name.

Matti's friend was a few years older than us, and we were talking about body piercing and tattoos.
Allen had lifted his top to show me his latest tattoo on his chest, the detail was incredible, a big lion head reaching from one side of his chest to the other.
I decided I wanted a tattoo but didn't know what I wanted.

'It hurts mind you' Allen said,

'I am hard-core, I am my father's punch bag, so pain doesn't bother me' I replied, now I knew they thought I was joking, but I wasn't.

My dad hit me almost every day, sometimes without reason, just because someone had annoyed him.
It was the first week in October, and I had finally started school, I was excited and was hoping that I would be in the same tutor group as I was when I was in the first year. The school pupils were divided into five groups with two different classes in each year group, I was in the yellow group, which was called Wilkinson house and I was put into the top group, I was hoping to be back in Miss Halts class, but as my grades were high, I was advised to join Mrs. Peacocks class instead.
After filling out the forms, I needed to complete I was taken to my new tutors. Mrs. Peacock was kind enough and was very welcoming towards me. She explained that with it being my last year, I would need to keep my head down. I guessed that comment was made because my school report would have mentioned me being expelled from Saint Dominic's.
I didn't say anything, I just sat at the back of the classroom and waited to be told were my first lesson was.

'Do you know where E block is?' she asked when the rest of the class left the room.

'Yes Miss, I used to be at this school in year seven' she looked at me straight in my eyes,

'Well get a move on, you don't want to be late' she continued

'In Ireland, you were in Technology, it is called system and control over here, you are in classroom E9.'
I grabbed my bag and coat and headed towards my class, I saw Mona in the corridor and stopped to say hello. Mona lived near me just at the back of my Nans, I had met her the week before, and she seems nice enough, she was excited to see me, and we agreed to meet up after school, so I could let her know how my day had gone.

Arriving outside my classroom, I peeped through the glass in the classroom door. I was sure I had made a mistake, this class was full of boys, and I didn't see one female in the whole class, so I opened the door slowly. The teacher noticed me standing in the doorway.

'You must be Sarah' he said, 'Please come in and take a seat. '

I looked at the floor, 'I wasn't sure I was in the right classroom' I said nervously as I entered the classroom.

My teacher pointed to the only seat available and asked if anyone in the class wanted to explain what we were doing in the lesson. A tall Asian boy put his hand up and walked over to my table.

'Hi Sarah, my name is Chesham, but everyone calls me Shas' he smiled

'I thought I was in the wrong class, I can't believe I am the only girl' I said giggling

'More attention' he whispered with a wink of the eye.

The lesson went well, and my next lesson was with Miss Halt, my old form teacher. I had been informed that she was married, and her name had changed to Mrs. Marsh. I was worried that my lesson would be awkward as I had never really learned French and I knew Mrs. Marsh was a French teacher. I sat down in class and noticed Anna, sat towards the end of the classroom, I waved at her, but she didn't wave back, so I wondered if she recognized me.

Feeling awkward I just sat down. A boy sat in front of me asked me what my name was. I told him, and he started mocking me, calling me an Irish bomber and asking ridiculous questions, like have I been trained up by the IRA and asking if I knew how to build a bomb. Rather than get upset and joined in.

'Yeah, I know how to build a bomb' I giggled 'We can't leave school in Ireland till we have mastered the pipe bomb at least' I replied with a big grin,

Bobby didn't know what to say and just turned back around in his chair.
Then Mrs. Marsh told me to be quiet as she wasn't going to let me disrupt her class. So, I sat in class, having no idea what she was saying in French, and as the end of the lesson, I was relieved to be getting out of her class.

My first day at school was good, and I had made a few friends, and caught up with old ones, so I was happy walking home. I realized I hadn't needed to worry about going back to the Ab dab, and everyone was pleasant enough.

That evening I spent most of my time with Alan, we were listening to music and catching up on our day. I had told Alan all about my day, while he waited on me hand and foot. He was doing my head in a bit fussing around me, and I had to snap at him a few times for acting weird. Secretly I loved the attention though, and for a change, it was nice attention, not like the unwanted attention I knew I was getting at home. I knew while we still lived at Nan I was safe, and dad couldn't even get away with looking at me the wrong way.

It was the next day, I was in the first lesson, and I was in English, I had been doodling on my book, just childish girly stuff like butterflies and hearts. The girl sat beside me was doodling too; she had drawn a tribal heart with her boyfriend's name inside. So, I wrote Alan's name on my doodle with a big smiley face next to it.

'Who is Alan?' the girl drawing beside me asked

'Just a boy, who lives near me' I replied,

'Do you like him?' she smirked

'He seems nice enough but its early days' I replied
'Well, I hope you don't mean Lynette's man, or she will skin you alive' she said getting up from her seat.

She walked towards the back of the classroom and whispered in a girl's ear, they were both looking at me and sniggering at each other, then the doodling girl came back to her seat and slammed her hand on my book.

'You want to watch yourself, little girl, Lynette is pissed' she whispered staring me in the eyes.

'But. I don't even know her' I said defending myself

'Don't mouth at me bitch or I will have you an all' she said shaking her head 'silly little girl, silly, silly little girl' she said condescendingly.

I had heard rumors that Lynette was a crazy cow when someone had pissed her off, I never for one moment thought that she would want to get at me, so I decided that break time to find her and explain the big misunderstanding. After all, I had been in the school as day surely, she would listen to me, but first I needed to know what her problem was. That break time I walked to the tennis courts looking for her, but I didn't see any sign of her or the group of girls, but I did notice Anna at the bottom of the courts smoking so I walked down to her, when I got closer she looked shifty.

'Are you okay?' I asked

'Nothing, just para that I will get caught smoking this joint, you okay' she asked.

I explained that I was in a bit of bother with Lynette, and I told her what I thought the reason was; Anna looked worried for me and said I needed to keep my head down and hopefully, it would all blow over. That put me at ease, and I had some of her joint to calm my nerves before heading back towards the school building. Just as I got to the top of the steps at the other end of the tennis courts, I noticed Lynette storming towards me with four girls in tow.

I tried just to walk past but she clocked me and started shouted, she was calling me a cheap, dirty slag, and she was yelling loud enough for a small circle of people has surrounded me.

She was shouting in my face that I was hitting on her man; I had no idea what she was going on about until she started screaming about a tattoo, and then the penny dropped. Her boyfriend was with Matti in his kitchen, and he showed me his tattoo. She got the wrong end of the stick and before I knew it I was dragged on the floor and she was booting me as hard as she could in the face. I tried to cover my head but two of the girls held my arms up above my face as each boot hit me in the head I screamed in pain, until finally, I heard one of the teachers Mrs. Waters shouting.

Lynette stopped beating me but then her friends booted me a few times before getting dragged away by the crowd that had formed around me.

Mrs. Waters pushed past the group and helped me to my feet, she ordered Lynette, and her two friends, to go and sit outside her office and screamed at the rest of the pupils to go back to class, as I got to my feet she was shaking her head at me.

'Not the best start now is it Sarah?' she said as we walked back towards the school.

My face hurt, and I couldn't answer, so I just looked up at her disapproving face. The look in her eyes said it all to me, as far as Mrs. Waters was concerned it was my fault, she seemed more annoyed that my beating had caused her to lose out on her staffroom gossip.

I had seen the school nurse and been sent home as she was concerned I might have had concussion, she the nurse rang my mum and I was told to wait in the nurse's office until she had arrived to collect me.

The time was dragging, and the school bell had gone off for lunchtime just as my mum turned up. The look of horror on my mum's face said it all, my face was bruised and swollen, I could see the swelling out of the corner of my eye, but I hadn't looked in the mirror, so I only had my mum's reaction.

The nurse had already got my bag and coat ready, so I stood up to put my jacket on. As I raised my arms to put my arm in my sleeve a sharpshooting ran down my spine, mum could see the pain I was in, and she shook her head and took my coat from me, I whimpered as my mum helped me put my arms through.

I was two days later when I would be forced to go back to school, and I was told to report straight to Mr. Wright's office, he was head of my year. As I sat outside the room, which was basically in the middle of the corridor, I wanted the ground to swallow me up. All the pupils walking past me seemed to stare that little bit longer than the typical curious looks, I felt like the whole school had been talking about me. When Mr. Wright emerged from his office to call me inside, I could see behind the door someone else in the office with him, as I got closer to the door I knew it was Lynette, the big platform shoes gave it away. Mr. Wright could sense my anxiousness and told me I would be fine. I sat in the chair beside her but didn't lift my head to look at her; I was ashamed at the state of my face if anything the bruising had become more noticeable in the two days and my whole forehead was covered in grey and yellow bruising.

My teacher had a better idea; he had told me to look straight at Lynette, so she could see what her anger had caused.

The trick worked as well, as soon as I looked up at her, the horror on her face was visible. She had tried to argue that it wasn't just her that had caused the damage to my face, but Mr. Wright was having none of it, he raised his voice and stood up behind his desk.

'The fact you got the other girls involved lies directly on your shoulders' he shouted 'Look at her Lynette; did she deserve such harsh treatment? He asked.

She shook her head and looked at the floor.

'I am ashamed to have such bullies in my school; you are lucky that Sarah doesn't want to press charges, I know I would if I was her!' he said as he sat back down behind his desk.

'You are both dismissed; now get to class while I decide what to do.'

Anything He Can Do, I Can Do Better...

It had been a few weeks since I had a beating off the girls, but Lynette had said sorry and realized she was completely in the wrong, she had opened up to me that she thought her boyfriend, who was also called Alan, but with two Ls, had been cheating on her and she had only got so angry as she had found out she was pregnant with Allan's baby. I was always the forgiven type anyway, but the fact that she took the time to come and at least explain was good enough for me.

We had also moved out of my Nans house, into our own property a few doors away. It was that close that we could see each other's front door. My cousin Wayne had started to come around to our house a lot, he would have a drink with my dad, and smoke loads of cannabis with him.
My dad smoked a lot anyway, and as far back as I remembered always smoked, it was only in the recent years that I knew what he was smoking as I was smoking it myself with my mates on the odd occasion someone could afford it.
I loved it when Wayne was at my house, because dad acted differently in front of other people, to the outside world we must have looked like an ordinary family, and apart from the daily beating and regular sexual abuse I had to cope with, we were normal enough.

As the weeks and months went on my relationship with Wayne changed, at the time, I thought in a good way, but I was completely wrong.

My Life in His Hands

Wayne started treating me like I was special, we would spend a lot of time in his bedroom practicing dance moves and having a good giggle, and I looked forward to spending more time with him. One day we were in his bedroom, my Nan was out in town with my mum and her sister, so he and I had the whole house to ourselves which he had pointed out. We had gone downstairs and made our way into the kitchen, so I could make a drink, as we walked past the front door, he had locked it which I thought was strange, but I didn't say anything.
Then in the kitchen, I felt his hand rush against my bum, so I moved out of the way.

He didn't say anything and just looked at me; awkwardly I looked back and asked if he wanted a cup of tea.

'I want a lot more than tea' he said laughing, me being a naïve teenager I just laughed the comment off.

We were in the living room, and he called me over to where he was sitting, asking me lots of questions about my dad, which seemed strange.

It was as if he knew the answers before I had a chance to reply, by the end of our twenty-minute conversation, it was clear that he knew my dad was abusing me.

I opened up a little and told him a few things, but from the look on his face, even though he knew about me being hit, he had no idea about the sexual abuse I was going through. Tears filled my eyes, as the abnormality of the situation hit me. I was scared that he would say something to my dad.

He then beckoned me to sit on his knee, so he could comfort me and reassured me that my secret was safe with him.

'I am sure this won't help' he said looking at me

'You are beautiful, and I am not saying it is an excuse, but I can see why someone would want to show you that attention.'

That comment should have rung alarms in my head, but it didn't. I cuddled into my cousin and tried to explain how powerless I was to stop my mentally ill father from treating me the way he did. He wiped the tears from my face and told me I was special, then he lent down to kiss me on the cheek, my body froze, and I just looked into space, I wasn't scared like I was when my dad kissed me, but more nervous than anything.

It was that moment that I realized I had a crush on my older family member, and I think he knew that too. As the weeks continued, my crush had become stronger, and our relationship has grown more flirtatious as a result. apparently when we were on our own only, and I knew deep down that it was all fucked up and that he was my relative, but I didn't care.

When Wayne finally lent down to kiss me, I let him. I had told myself that I wouldn't let it get any further than that and after the kiss, I had become awkward around him. He apparently noticed this tension and said we could forget all about it and go back to how things were before it got awkward. Naturally, I agreed, but things didn't go back to how they were, as it happened, I and my cousin spent a lot less time together and only really seen each other when he was visiting my dad.

Things at home started getting bad as well; my dad knew I smoked cannabis so if any went missing, I was the first person to be blamed.

My dad sold the stuff, so the house was always full of random people buying drugs from him. I wasn't stupid, I would never have stolen off the monster that I called my dad, through fear of being caught, but even my innocence couldn't help. It was mid-winter, Christmas has been and gone, and my dad had a quarter of an ounce of cannabis go missing. Of course, it was me who had taken it, even though the house was full of teenagers that morning. They would never steal from my dad because they had respect, this was something my dad always shouted at me for, the lack of respect I gave him.

I had started crying because I knew what was coming but that made him even angrier. In his eyes, I was causing a scene in front of his mates, so he dragged me into the living room by my ponytail and started hitting around the back of the head.

I just took it as normal, and when he had finished unleashing his rage on his petite fifteen-year-old daughter, he calmly walked back into the kitchen and carried on playing cards with his mates, which included my cousin.

Weeks had turned into months, and Wayne had started giving me smoke and telling me not to let my dad know, which I had agreed. I had been going through a rough time. It was spring 2000 I was preparing for my GSCEs. Which seemed pointless as I had basically missed out on a year at school. I didn't have the time to complete my coursework like all the other pupils in my year, so I knew my grades would be low, but I wasn't the type of person to give up, so I had spent most of my time in my bedroom revising. I remember my dad walking into my bedroom and telling me to tidy up my room.

'I will when I have finished this' I said pointing to my paperwork

'You will do it now' he shouted

'But... I' I replied and with that my dad had gone into a rage and started throwing my belonging around my room

'Stop it, you are ruining my work' I shouted, but that just made him worse.

Then he had told me to get out of his house, so I grabbed my coat and ran past him, straight down the stairs and out the front door.

Ironically Wayne was just about to knock on mine and instead followed me to find out what was wrong, once out of view from my house, I had explained to Wayne what had happened.

'You look like you need a smoke, fancy coming for a walk?' he asked.

To be honest, I had no other plans so decided it was an excellent idea, I was so angry with my dad that a smoke seemed perfect.

So, we headed down towards rough park which was at the bottom of our estate, we walked straight through the park and across the train track at the bottom, the train track was only used twice a day with a train traveling to the power plant with coal, so crossing the trail was easy. We found a quiet spot and sat down, he gave me the things I needed to make a joint and he has asked me about four times on the walk down if I wanted a sip of his coke, but I had declined.

We had a smoke, and I walked back to the estate in the other direction to Wayne, because I didn't want to be seen with him.

We started meeting up for half an hour every day that week, and each time he had offered me a drink of his coke. This time I had agreed because yet again I argued with my dad, this time over something the twins had done, but as usual I got the blame.

Wayne had just passed me a very strong joint, I was coughing so he asked me if I wanted I drink, I said no, but he asked me again about ten minutes later while I was making the joint and I had agreed. Taking a big drink from the bottle, I had commented that it tasted flat. After I had smoked through my throat was dry, and I ended up drinking most of his coke to myself, I had offered the bottle back, but he said I could finish it. Wayne then started making another joint, but I was already spaced out.

'I think I am stoned already' I said smiling

'Is it starting to take effect?' he replied,

'I will make this one weaker than the last, then shall I?' he asked.

I nodded my head and lay down on the grass. My head felt all fuzzy, and my body seemed heavy.
My body was telling me something was wrong, and my mouth was so dry, so I sat up again, it felt like I was stiff, and I just manage to sit up and take a drink of coke from the bottle.

'I feel like shit' I said before lying back down

My Life in His Hands

'You will be fine, just relax. If you close your eyes I will make sure you get home okay' he replied,

I tried to respond but I didn't even have the strength to talk, so I closed my eyes, only for a few minutes.
When I opened them again I felt completely paralyzed, I couldn't move an inch or speak. I had started to panic, but Wayne was stroking my face telling me I was okay. I wanted to tell him how I was feeling but I couldn't move my mouth; it felt like it had been super glued shut.
Then I felt his hand on the top of my leg, he was rubbing his hand up and down the inside of my thigh and asking me if I liked it. I wanted to scream but I couldn't. I tried to move my hand to stop him, but I couldn't even feel my arms. I thought I was dying and I couldn't even say how I was feeling. His hand got higher up my leg, and he was rubbing me.

'I know you like that because you are getting all damp' he smiled and continued.

My trousers had been removed without me knowing and then he moved from my line of vision, all I could see was the trees swaying high above me, suddenly I felt his head between my legs as he started to lick me.

'I bet you like that too' he said, 'you let your dad do this to you so I guessed you wouldn't mind me doing it, and anything he can do, I can do a whole lot better.'

I felt like I was going to be sick, my mouth was filling up with water, but I couldn't even turn my head to the side. I was like a solid piece of stone on the ground, with only the bird above being able to see what was happening to me.
'I am going to go one step further, then your daddy though' he laughed.

When he returned into my vision, and I was trying my hardest to stare at him, so he knew this was wrong, he knew himself and carried on muttering to himself.

'This has been on the cards for a long time, you have been all over me, so I don't know what you expected' he said as I seen him unzipped his jeans.

It seemed like a spilled second by the time I felt him penetrate me, the numbness of my body was slowly wearing off and the pain I felt inside was more painful, he was far from gentle, and it dawned on me that I was being raped. I was the fifteen, and he was twenty-four and he had planned this for a long time was the words that rang in my head. When he had finished, he had a big grin on his face and laughed.

'Well now I feel special' he said, 'you let me go further than daddy.'

Water filled my mouth, and I had started to be sick, Wayne turned me onto my side, and as I was vomiting, I realized I was getting movement back in my right arm and my left leg which seemed weird.
I tried to talk, but still, the words wouldn't come out of my mouth.

'When you are feeling up to it I will take you home, think you smoked too much don't you?' he asked.

'Still not talking, oh okay I don't mind the silent treatment, you talk too much anyway' he continued.
'We best keep this to ourselves now. we don't want me telling you dad about the hideous lies you have been telling about him now do we?'

My Life in His Hands

It seemed like hours I had been lying on the floor, and when I finally was able to speak, I let out all sorts of vile words to my cousin. I told him he was worse than my dad, and that my dad was mentally ill, so what was his excuse. His reply shocked me and changed me as a person.

'It is your fault now Sarah, with your flirty laugh and adoring looks, you gave me permission love, all men will be the same, it is not our fault you are a cheap tart who wants cock. That is all your fault you were asking for it' he turned to me 'What was I meant to do, just let you flirt and not get anything back?'

I hated him 'You make me sick' I said in disgust

'No that's the drugs you took lovey, good, aren't they?'

I tried to get up, but he pushed me back down.
He was shaking his head and had told me to wait a little longer, but I just needed to get away.
I had feeling again in my body, but it was more like pins and needles rather than the numbness I had experienced earlier on.
After he had threatened me and warned me what would happen if I told anyone, he finally gave me my trousers to put back on and commented about next time we will pick better weather.
'There won't be the next time you sick fucking prick' I snapped.

'I am the sick fuck; you are the one who sucks your own dad's cock lovey, I think you will find you are the sick twisted fuck up, not me. I am just taking what was offered to me. Can I ask you something before I take you home? '

How dare he I thought, 'No fuck off and stay away from me' I shouted,

'Calm down, or I am going to have to shut you up' he warned 'I was only gonna ask why your daddy don't put his cock inside you?' he smiled.

'Fuck you. You are scum. I would never let anyone do that to me' I snapped

'Raise your voice at me again, and you will never talk again, you say you would never let anyone do that, so I must be the special one eh? Was it your first time?' he asked.

'No, please just leave me alone' a tear fell down my cheek,

'See so why are you complaining. Not as if I broke you or anything' he said pulling me up to my feet

'I will take you home now, remember not a word this is our little secret, and you are good at keeping them, I know.'

Once we got to the front of my house, he had decided that he should walk in first and that I hover outside the house for a few minutes. That suited me because I wanted to be on my own anyway.

As he walked towards my front door, he turned back towards me and told me to remember what he had said. How could I not remember, the sick bastard had made me feel like a cheap tart as he said and convinced me that all the abuse in my life was my own fault because of the way I acted.

I felt sick, and after a few minutes, I walked down towards my house. My body was still really weak, and I was out of breath, my heart was beating fast, and my stomach was cramping up bad, so when I got through the door, I made my way straight upstairs to my bedroom.
I opened the door, and the room was trashed, just then I remembered why I went out in the first place and wished I had stayed at home, in a weak moment of my mind I realized that what my dad did to me was nothing compared to the ordeal I had experienced that afternoon.

I lay on my bed in a ball and sobbed as quietly as possible so not to be heard downstairs. I fell asleep listening to the two monsters having a laugh and a joke downstairs. These monsters were part of my family. That made me even more convinced that I bring all this shit onto myself by acting like a slag.

Time to Speak Up...

Wayne had started to spend even more time with my dad, which was good for me because dad acted differently in front of most people. My dad was always off his face on drugs which also helped. Crack cocaine was his new-found friend, and even though he and my mum tried to hide it from me I wasn't stupid, they were both heavily addicted to this expensive drug, so dad needed to sell more cannabis to fund his habit. Mum was sent out to work and was even told by my dad that she had to come home with enough money to buy some rocks, which is what they called the crack in front of us kids.

Mums wages weren't that good so she would have to steal from the till to have the two hundred pounds needed for their daily addiction. If she came home, empty-handed dad would take his frustration out on all of us, so it was in mum's interest to make sure she got generous tips, by flirting with the punters, shortchanging them and dipping into the till each evening.

One day during that time, sticks in my head, Wayne, and my dad would buy cannabis together, and as Wayne could only smoke it at my house, it would stay with my dad until he was back around, which seem like all day every day.

I had come to hate him almost as much as I despised my father. Wayne would make excuses to get me on my own for a few minutes at a time to warn me about speaking out about what had happened that spring.

I couldn't tell anyone without making myself sound wrong anyway, and as if I would tell my mother anything. I told her about my dad, and it seemed like I wasn't believed, I had told my auntie Amy too, and she called me a liar. It was bad enough me judging myself without anyone else doing it for me. So, I promised to keep it to myself.

That afternoon Wayne had gone back to my Nans earlier than usual, I remember my dad commenting on him acting strange, but I thought nothing of it and went out to see if Mona was about. It was cold and raining so I didn't stay out long, and I knew my mum was due home by six at the latest that evening, so just after six, I headed back home with Mona in tow. As we approached the front of my house we could hear my dad screaming and shouting at my mum, she had apparently not come home with enough money to feed his nasty drug habit, and as usual, it was my entire mums fault in his eyes. I turned to Mona and advised her to turn around because I knew dad would take his anger out on everyone.

'Why the hell are you going in?' she asked,

'Stay out for a bit till he calms the fuck down.'

I replied with 'I can't, if I don't go home now he will kick off ten times more.'
After a few minutes of trying to talk me round. Mona finally gave up, and we arranged to meet up again the next day, she had said I needed to tell her what happens and that if it got too bad, I could stay at hers. She had spoken to her mum in the past, and she had always said I could sleep but I never took her up on her offer.
Walking closer towards my front door I noticed the house had seems quieter; maybe dad had stopped bitching, I thought to myself.

When I walked in dad was sat at the kitchen table with his head in his hands and mum was stood looking out of the window, staring into space.

'You okay' I asked as I walked into the kitchen, but neither of them answered

'Good day at work mum?' I said raising my voice slightly as to make sure I was heard.

Mum turned around to look at me, her face was blotchy, and her eyes were all puffed up from all the crying, and dad just puts his head up and muttered something which I didn't make out. The tension in that room was bad, and I felt uneasy, I made my excuses and went up to my room.

Within minutes I was called downstairs as dad bellowed my name through the house. Mum wasn't in the kitchen at this point, so I asked where she was.
'I told her to take the boys to Nans, why?' he asked, I had no idea, I just shrugged my shoulders, dad had gone on to explain that he was pissed off because his cannabis had gone missing, and he demanded it back.

I told him I hadn't seen it which was the truth, but he started pushing me about and calling me a liar.
I was adamant I hadn't seen it which made him see red. I was pushed onto the living room floor, banging my back off the table as I hit the ground.

'You have two seconds to tell me where it is or I am going to beat it out of you!' he screamed.

'Please dad, I promise I haven't seen it, I am telling the truth' I begged to wipe the snot dripping from my nose mixed with the waterfall of tears that drenched my face

'You are a lying fucking bitch.'

He pulled me up just to pin me against the wall.
He was forcing me to look at him as his nose almost
touched mine and warned me that he was going to hurt
me, he then started hitting me around the head and
shouting 'liar, liar' repeatedly with every bang to the back
of my head.
He then stepped back as I fell in a heap on the floor.

'I am going to your nans, you have five minutes to find it,
or you know what will happen, I just showed you' he said
as he walked out of the room.

I was shaking uncontrollably, I knew for a fact I hadn't
taken anything, but I also knew it was in my best interest
to try and find it. I wiped my face with my already wet
sleeve and pulled myself up using the table. I was
frantically looking under every surface of the room, in case
the cannabis had just been dropped, but it was nowhere to
be found.

I had just started looking down the back of the sofa when I
heard the front door open again.

'Please dad, I have looked everywhere I can't find it' I
begged, bursting into tears again.

'I warned you to find it; no one else would have taken it.
So, I know it was you.'

I pleaded 'It wasn't I promise you' he scared straight at
me,

'You have two minutes to find it' he shouted.

I turned my back to him and carried on looking down the back of the sofa, I could feel him getting closer to me, my legs started to shake, and I thought I was going to get a beating, but he just punched me in the arm and pushed me out of the way.

'Do you think I am stupid' he asked. 'I have already looked there?'

He walked out of the room holding his head, almost pulling his hair from his scalp. I heard a big bang in the kitchen, and then the kitchen draws open.

I panicked, I knew the Wilkinson Sword knife was in that drawer, and it was the top draw that opened. That is one thing this point in my life had changed about me, I was so much more aware of sounds and movements, and I listened for every detail, convinced that he had that knife in his hands when he walked back into the living room I closed my eyes and screamed.

'Stupid bitch shut the fuck up' he said rushing up to me and grabbed me from behind, he then put his hand around my mouth. I looked her straight in the eyes hoping that he would snap out of this fucked up angry mode he was in but all it did was make him more pissed off.

He pushed me to the ground and calmly sat on the sofa. He then pointed to the living room door and told me to shut it. I was shaking at this point, and he started laughing at me and telling no child of his would steal from him, and that I was to stand by the TV when I had closed the door. I knew it was best to do as he said; I stood where he had pointed to and looked down at the floor. By this point, I knew he didn't have the knife in his hand, and it was just my mind worrying me. In comparison, what happened next was minor, but still was bad.

My Life in His Hands

I was ordered to turn out my pocket, which I did. Then I was told to get undressed, I tried to argue but that was making him mad again, and I was already very sore from him hitting me and pushing me about, so I started to get undress.

It was chilly, and I had removed my jumper and trousers and threw them in his direction as ordered. He picked my trousers up and was patting the pocket area; he then looked up at me stood with my socks, knickers, and t-shirt.

'Did I tell you to stop, fucking strip!' he demanded.

'Why I have no more pockets you can see I don't have your smoke' I pleaded

'You think I don't know where women hide things; I want it all off you dirty slag.'

I didn't want to get naked in front of this dirty monster, but I knew I had no choice, so I did what I was told. I was stood completely naked with my childlike fifteen-year-old underdeveloped body and naturally used my hands to cover the most private part of my body.
Dad stood up and screamed that I was to remove my hands, he got close to me and started examining my vagina to determine whether I had hidden his precious smoke inside me, which to me sounded like a ridiculous thing anyone would do.

Once satisfied that I hadn't buried it inside me, he walked out of the room and told me to get dressed, calling me all sorts of names in the process.

Ten minutes later mum had walked through the door, I was dressed and sat on the stairs with my head leaning against the banister, and she walked straight over to me.

'What has he done?' She whispered.

I didn't need to tell her, she could tell by my face, and I think that was enough for her, she gave me a nod of the head and advised me to go to my room before my dad got back. So, I did. I heard the twins and Matthew downstairs, but I hadn't listened to my dad walk back in the house. Just then I heard my mum walking up the stairs; I knew it was her because she coughed when she was about four steps up, from the bottom. She walked into my room, and I was expecting her to ask if I was okay.

'What has happened between you and Wayne?' she asked tried to look at her confused and asked her what she meant.

'Something has happened, because he said that he stole your dads smoke and asked me to give it to you, so your dad stopped slapping you, now why would he do that?' she asked.

'I don't know why he would have done that.' I replied

'Has Wayne done something, Sarah please I just need to know' she pleaded.

I shook my head, but she could tell I was hiding something and told me that she thought I needed to let her know before my dad found out.
Mum had also said that she would sort the smoke situation out with my dad and that I was best to stay in my room for the rest of the evening.

She surprised me when she lent down and kissed me on the forehead.

The next day, as usual, my dad had acted as nothing had happened, he was sat at the kitchen table rolling himself a joint, with the lump of smoke that had caused all of yesterday's drama. 'Morning love' he said smiling, politely. I had said my good mornings, made myself and dad a cup of tea and went upstairs to get ready for school, as I was getting undressed and into my uniform, when I caught a glimpse in the mirror of the bruising all over my back.

I also had a few small bruises on my arm and another on the top of my thigh. I looked a mess, but in the same breath, I had started to get used to having to keep covered up to hide the marks made by that monster. It was during school that day that I realized Wayne had planned for me to get into so much trouble, I don't think he understood how badly I would be punished, but after thinking about it all day, I felt that it was his way of keeping some control over me.

Like a statement that he can cause my home life to become even worse if he wanted to, I was angry and was snappy at everyone that day, even my music teacher, and he took no shit and sent me straight to Mr. Wrights office who was surprised to see me.
I had only been to his office in the past if I had been sent on an errand for a teacher or the get help or advise if I was struggling.

Mr. Wright had asked me what the problem was, and I just told him I had been having a stressful day and made an excuse that my younger brothers had me up all night as they were ill.

I hated lying, but I had been up all night, I couldn't sleep as I was worried my dad would have kicked off again, but I couldn't tell my teacher that obviously.

Later that day when I had got home from school, only mum and the boys were in the house, I had asked where my dad was and much to my surprise, my mum had said he was out at the pub. Dad never went out, only to the local shop for his Budweiser and to the bookies to put on his bets. I had asked why he had gone to the pub and mum just said because he was an adult and that's what adults do. Something just really didn't sit right, I had a feeling it would all turn out wrong, but I never expected what was to come next.

It was about eight o'clock in the evening, and I heard my dad walking in with my Uncle Patrick and Uncle Matthew. They walked straight into the living room and stood in front of the fireplace in a line. Dad turned the TV off and put the remote on the table along with his bottle of Budweiser and then called my mum in from the kitchen, where she was sat reading her magazine.

'Laura! in here now' he snapped as she walked into the room

'Close the door' Matthew said to her

'What's going on' mum asked my uncle, Matt

'As you know, we all went to the pub for a drink; now we are not stupid even though she thinks we are' Matt replied looking directly at me.

I looked at my mother and then back at my uncle slightly confused and asked what he meant; then dad started talking

'We know something had happened between you and your dirty prick of a cousin, but just answer me one thing?' dad said.

I started crying, and my Uncle Matt said 'Just be honest Sarah, you are not the one in trouble here, and he is for fuck sake. You are a child, and he is almost twenty-seven.'

Dad told me to look at him, so I did

'Did he have sex with you?' he asked, I just looked at the floor, crying heavily by this point. 'You do know he is a pedophile if he has?' dad said ironically.

By this point my mum's sister Eliza had walked into the room, My Uncle Patrick must have told her. She sat down beside me and asked what was going on, but I was too emotional to speak. Micky then asked me again.

'Did he have sex with you Sarah, yes or no?

I nodded my head, and before I knew it, my dad had picked up his beer and him and Micky had walked out of the house.
I heard dad saying that he was going to kill him as the front door slammed. They were on their way to my Nans.

Nan opened the door, and my dad had walked past her and straight to the living room to confront Wayne, he was adamant that it was all me, and that I was coming on to him all the time.
My dad was about to leave and was shouting Wayne to come outside, but as he got to the front door, my dad smashed the bottle clean around his head.
While this was going on, I had explained to my mum and aunt what had happened the day of the rape, and the

threats I had been given since.

Mum asked what had started it and I explained about the crush I had on him and that I was always flirting with him and that it was my fault. It was only my fault for telling him get away with doing what my dad was doing to me, in his eyes that permitted him to treat me the same, and in some respects a whole lot worse than my dad ever did.

I was upset, so I didn't go into too much detail, the details would all come out later.

Tried and Tested...

`   The evening that everything had come out about Wayne and that night seemed to drag on forever. My prick of a cousin had been taken to hospital for stitches to his head, and the police had arrested my dad, and I was waiting to be interview by the police myself. It was about two in the morning when mum finally told me to go to bed and as soon as my head hit the pillow I was fast asleep.

The next morning, I had been woken by the sound of the twins arguing outside my bedroom door.
I shouted at them to be quiet and then I heard mum shout up to me that I needed to get up anyway. Reluctantly I got up and went to the bathroom. Once washed and dressed I walked downstairs which seemed quiet, I peeped my head around the living room door, but the room was empty. I then walked past the back door and seen mum hanging out the washing and the boys playing nicely together for a change. It was a lovely day outside, but I still wished I was back in bed. I opened the back door to ask mum if she wanted a cup of coffee, she had said yes but told me to make Micky a drink as he was on his way around.
I thought it was early until I walked into the kitchen to put the kettle on and was shocked to see it was almost twelve. I made the drink and put them on the table just as mum walked into the kitchen. She looked up at the clock.

'I know I should have been awake ages ago' I said to her

'No, it not that' she replied, 'I am surprised your dad isn't home by now, they released him over two hours ago.'

She looked at me and said, 'You are going to have to press charges.'

'I just want to leave it' I explained.

'You can't just leave it, it is wrong, and you know it is, plus he has pressed charges on your dad, so you need to whether you like it or not' she snapped

'But I just want to forget about it.'

She shook her head at me, 'He needs to pay for what he did to you.'

That annoyed me, 'What like dad' I snapped.

'Fuck sake, that is different, and you know it is!' she snapped back at me, I had hit a nerve.

'Dad is just as bad' I replied with tears in my eyes.
'Your dad was only the once and he must live with that, and this is rape Sarah not a flash of skin when you were a kid, there is a lot of differences' she said defending him.

'Just once, you know that isn't true, and it was a lot more than a flash of skin' I replied disgusted at the way she had to describe my horror story.

She stormed out of the room and said she didn't need to listen to this shit. 'This Shit' was my life, and I felt like she didn't even care.

It was later that day when the police turned up to question me, I knew they were on their way as they had told my mum to expect them, but it didn't stop the nerves as the male and female officers led me into the living room.

My Life in His Hands

My heart was pumping fast, and my hands were all
clammy. After I had told the female officer what had
happened, the male policeman informed me that I was
making a serious accusation and asked if I understood the
severity of what I was saying. That just made me feel like
they didn't believe me; they then asked me to remain in
the living room while they spoke to my mum. When they
finish they knocked on the door before walking back into
the room, mum was with them, and the female officer
went on to explain that generally in cases like mine. The
person would need to go for a medical, so they could use
it as evidence if it went to court. She said I would get a
letter through the post with an appointment and a leaflet
to explain what the medical exam would entail.

Then just as they were leaving they had asked if I wanted
to add anything to my statement, I told them I didn't, and
they left. Within minutes I had my coat on and was ready
to go out, mum was quiet, and the atmosphere was tense, I
wasn't in the mood for it, so I decide to try and track Mona
down.

She was at the park with a few people we knew; you could
tell they had been sat they're a while by the empty beer
bottles around them, when I got closer, she looked up at
me with her stoned eyes and past me the joint in her hand.

'You will need a light' she said as she passed it to me

'I have needed a light for ages' she laughed.

I was hoping to get her on her own, so I could tell her
what had happened the past few days but she was too out
of it that there was no point in even wasting my breath,
she wouldn't remember it in the morning.

Mona wasn't a big smoker really, but when she did, she would smoke till she would pass out and be sick and I wasn't really in the mood to be looking after her, so I told her I was only out for an hour and then I was in for the night. She didn't care really; she was too busy demanding that one of the boys make another joint and save her twos on it.

After having a smoke, I headed back home, but Barry a friend of ours offered to walk me home. He was flirting the whole way home, and it annoyed me because he only acted like that when no one else was around.

As if, he was embarrassed by me or something, so once we got by the shop and only few hundred yards from my house I stopped, and I asked him straight
'why did he act ashamed of me in front of his mates.'
He didn't have an answer so I told him to leave me alone and I walked the rest of the way home on my own.

Dad was finally home when I got back, and he had told me to sit down at the kitchen table, so I could explain everything to him in detail. It made my skin crawl, not only because of the nature of the conversation but because it was him who I had to explain it all too. After repeating myself for over an hour I went upstairs to go to bed, mum had pointed out that I hadn't eaten all day, but I didn't care, I just wanted that day to end.

I was a week later before I got my letter for the appointment with the court's medical team.

The leaflet went into detail about the examination I had to have done, which made me sick to the stomach just reading the words; I was dreading the week later when my appointment was booked for me.

My Life in His Hands

Mum had explained that the doctor would insert something inside me to determine whether I had been involved in sexual activity and she told me from personal experience that it was not going to be pleasant in any way. Nothing about my life was pleasant, but this was something I needed to prepare myself for, so I spent most of that week in my bedroom waiting for this horrible appointment to arrive.

The day of the appointment, I was feeling unwell. Mum had said it was because of nerves, but she told me that it would be over in minutes and that I just needed to try and put my mind off things. The whole morning seemed to drag, and by the time lunchtime came there was no way I could stomach any food, so mum made lunch for the boys and me, and she set off into town to get our bus. The appointment was booked at the local hospital which took almost an hour to get to, so even though my appointment wasn't till three o'clock, we had set off just after one to make sure we were on time. I was just glad to be going, in my head the quicker I left the house that day, the quicker it was over.

The examination was as horrendous as I expected, I was given a hospital gown to put on and asked to remove my underwear, I was then told to lie on the bed with my legs open while the doctor placed different thing inside me. I never knew the results myself, and when I asked what would happen next, the doctor said the result got sent straight to the courthouse where the prosecutors and defense would have them as evidence.

I felt like a piece of meat afterward, and I hurt inside where the doctor wasn't a gentle as I am sure he could have been, I honestly felt like this was all part of the punishment.
A punishment I had convinced myself I was deserving of.

When mum and I had returned home, dad had informed us that the court case was scheduled for the end of the following week and that because I was still a minor, I wouldn't have to stand up in court.
I would do a video link in the building next door to the old courthouse. The relief was hard to explain, I had never seen a courtroom in real life, I had only seen them on TV but I had heard about them, and I had heard how the prosecutors treat people, so I was glad not to be put through all that.

Dad had continued the conversation and said that my cousin Katie had accused Wayne of doing the same to her. In all honesty, I did not believe her for one minute. This is the same girl who had her mum's boyfriend and her granddad in trouble with lies before. I was angry with her, and it showed

'That's bollocks' I snapped

'Why do you say that?' mum asked

'Because she didn't even see Wayne never mind have anything happen to her' I replied.

'Well the police have considered it, and she is doing a video link too' my dad replied.

Dad then went on to explain that, as Katie and I were both making accusations against the same person we weren't allowed near each other till after the court case. Which suited me down to the ground, I felt like she was taking the piss out of my situation by making a false claim.
On the other hand, I did start to think that maybe she was telling the truth, Wayne had been able to keep me quiet, so perhaps he had some hold on her as well.

The day before the video link dad had started acting strangely; he was being over kind to me and checking up on me all the time. I had spent most of the week in my bedroom listening to my music when I wasn't at school doing my GCSEs.

Not that I cared whether I passed my exams or not, too much was going on in my life for me to give a shit about my future, I just needed to get over this week, and that was hard enough. I was terrified of the video link, but I wasn't going to let on. What happens if they call me a liar? I thought.

I didn't know how I would react, so I had all the different scenarios in my head to help me deal with the questions I was going to be asked the next day. By this point, I must have repeated myself over twenty times to different people that I had started questioning myself about the whole ordeal. I cannot explain adequately how ill all the stress was making me feel, but when dad was nice, it was turning my stomach.

Maybe he realized how wrong he had been, but that was just wishful thinking on my part.
The truth was my dad was scared stiff that if I could go through this with Wayne then maybe I would speak up about him as well.

My proof of this came later that evening when mum was bathing the boys ready for bed. I was sat in the kitchen reading some notes for my exam the following week. I hadn't even noticed dad walk in the room until he was stood right beside me. He lent down with his face as close to mine as he could without touching me and hissed in my face.

'You dare mention me tomorrow, and I will make sure you come home in a box.'

I looked up at him; he had that evil glint in his eyes again and repeated himself, but this time in a firmer voice. I told him I wouldn't say anything and he sat down in the chair opposite me, and just kept staring at me. I put my head down as if to carry on reading when he demanded I look up at him, so I did as I was ordered.

'I am coming with you tomorrow, because I don't trust you' he said,

'I won't say anything dad' I said defending myself

'I know you fucking won't because I will be there with you to make sure' he replied, and with that, I closed my books and organized my papers.

I then got up to make my way back to my bedroom where I could revise in peace, without the evil stare of my dad putting me off. As I walked past him though he grabbed the top of my arm, and looked me deep in the eye.

'I am just warning you' he said before pushing me away in the act of disgust.

That evening I had gone to bed early, not that I could sleep. My mind was working overtime, and I could help but feel an almighty dread. The quicker I was asleep, the quicker all this would be over, but that just seemed to make me struggle to settle even more. It must have been about eleven at night when I heard my mum come up the stairs, she peeped round my doorway, and I turned around, so she knew I wasn't asleep yet.

'You have a long day ahead of you tomorrow, so you best go to sleep' she whispered,

'Trust me, mum, I am trying.'

The next morning, I felt like I was going to throw up, mum had made me a cup of tea and some toast and called me down the stairs. I only managed to eat half of my toast and a sip of my drink by the time I ran to the toilet a removed the contents of my stomach.

'You will be grand once we get going' dad had shouted through the toilet door.

I stood in the toilet for what seemed like ages but, it was only a few minutes that had passed, I was staring at myself in the mirror, conscious that I was feeling weak and dizzy.

I had told myself in my head that in another few hours it would all be over and I could finally put it behind me.

That had given me the motivation I needed to go back upstairs and get myself ready. Once I was dressed and had brushed my hair, we were prepared to leave. Mum had wished me luck and me, and my dad had set off to catch our bus.
My dad and I didn't speak the whole way to the courthouse, I didn't want to talk anyway, and dad was his usual mental self, he hated being in public anyway but sitting on a bus with lots of people were apparently getting at him. He was shifty, playing with his hands and shaking his knee.
That was always a sign that he felt uncomfortable.

If mum were with us, she would have calmed him down, but this weak side amused part of me to him.

I felt like I could take control if I needed to and for me, this was a new feeling.

I realized that I wasn't as scared of him anymore and that all it would take is one little line in this trial, which could open the can of worms.

I knew I needed to be careful with what I was going to say, but in my head, all I could hear was Wayne saying to me that 'if your dad can do it to you, then I can do it better.'

I knew in Wayne's mind that was the main reason for him raping me, not that it was an excuse, nothing can excuse that sort of behavior, but I understood.

In my eyes, this all started when I was nine years old, and the person who was responsible was fidgeting like an awkward child beside me and for once in my life, which made me feel powerful.

Once we had arrived at the courthouse, the female police officer that had first interviewed me was stood outside waiting, dad and I walked over, and she asked how I was feeling.
I said I was okay even though I wasn't at all. She then explained that everyone was already in court and that I was to follow her through the round to the building as the side of the courts, she said I wouldn't need to see anyone and that I would be in and out before the courtroom was released. As soon as she told me that it was as if a huge weight had been lifted off my shoulders.
We walked in a side door, and the corridor was long and narrow with bright white walls, there were three doors on each side, and the first entry we were shown into was a small office, where we were asked to wait so the officer could tell the staff we had arrived.

I was shaking, and my hands were clammy, now it was me who was acting like a fidgety child. A few minutes later the female officer had returned with another woman with her, she introduced herself as Jill, and she explained that she was the person who was going to ask me the questions.

We were then asked to follow her down the corridor. We were led into a smaller room, full of computers and a big screen. There was a middle-aged man sat behind the desk, and Jill had explained that this man was going to film the interview and send it to the courtroom. She then turns to my dad and told him this is where he can sit to watch his brave daughter being interviewed.
I had started to go dizzy but tried to put it to the back of my mine.

'Shall I show you which room we are in now?' she asked me. I just nodded back.

'Good luck love, I'll be watching you' I had my dad say as we left him in the room.

I knew it was a warning more than a comforting comment, but I just ignored him and went with Jill to the room where my interview was to take place.

When she opened the door and beckoned me in, I just stood and looked around me. The room looked like a children's nursery, all brightly colored pictures on the wall, drawn by young children. The seats were as small as the ones you would find in an infant school, and there were toys and books all around the room. Jill asked me to take a seat at the table, so I did.

On the table were lots of coloring pencils and crayons and a stack of paper, I looked down at it as I took my seat and Jill explained that generally if a child were in this room, she would make them draw pictures about their feeling.

'You are too old for that I am guessing?' she said with a smile

'I think so, yes' I replied

She locked the door and turned on the TV, that sat at the front of the room. There was a video camera attached to the top, and Jill had told me to try and ignore it, she said just imagine it is me and you and no one else.

'Just answer my questions the best you can and take your time, if you need me to stop at any time please just say so, and we will' she said.

I answered every question truthfully and honestly, but when it came to asking how I felt about it all, I couldn't explain. I said I didn't know how I felt and she looked at me confused.

'Surely you know how you feel' she said,
'Are you angry, upset what?'.

'Numb' was the only truthful answer I could give her.

I was questioned for over half an hour when Jill turned the TV back off.

'You are doing really, well Sarah, you should be proud of yourself' she said patting me on the back as we were leaving the interview room.

Dad was waiting in the corridor, and the pride Jill said I should have had was taken the second I seen him standing there with a big grin on his face, he put his arm around me and told me he was proud. At least he was, I just felt like a silly little tart that let dirty men do these horrible things to me. Dirty men who I should have been able to trust.
They say if you can't trust your dad then you can't trust anyone so, I didn't feel proud in any way.

As far as I was concerned, I had nothing to be proud of, apart from keeping daddy's dirty secret out of my interview.

Dad hadn't spoken to me the whole way home; I could see that the entire day had started to get to him and it was clear he needed a smoke. As soon as we got home I headed up to my bedroom, it was over an hour when my mum popped her head around my door to see if I was okay, but by then I was fast asleep.
The day had taken its toll on me.

Injustice...

The trial had been and gone, and all that was left to do was wait, and see what happened next. As it turned out Wayne had got away with what he had done to me, through lack of evidence. My cousin Katie was meant to do a video link with her statement, but she had dropped charges that day, which apparently made her look like she was making the whole thing up. Mum was convinced that because of this, it made me look like I was making up stories too. My dad also took the law into his own hands that evening and even though Wayne had told the paramedics that he had slept with his uncle's daughter, there was still no proof that I hadn't consented to it. Also, because it was months later by the time I had the medical examination, there were no traces of the drug he had used to sedate me when the rape took place.

Wayne had been ordered to stay away from Crosby, and my family. To me that wasn't good enough, I felt like I wasn't believed and that made me hate myself even more. I had finally started to feel proud that I had finally got through the court case to then be told that it was all a waste of time. That cut me deep.
I had started to go off the rails a bit, smoking, even more, cannabis and not giving a shit about anything or anyone, especially myself. I was made to feel like all this shit I had to deal with was brought on by myself and with my parents just wanting to sweep it under the carpet and forget about it, it made me angry at everyone.
I had gone to my Nan's one day and she acted so cold around me, so I asked her out right what was the problem and she said she was sad to see Wayne leave.

That really pissed me off, my own Nan taking his side as well. What was the point in anything anymore? I wished I had the strength to just fuck off somewhere where nobody knew me but I, was scared to leave home. I was coming up sixteen, and I had finally given up. There were a few occasions I had got so down that I had wondered what it would be like to take my own life, but they were just stupid thoughts I told myself until one day I got really close to doing something stupid.

I was out with Mona drinking most of the afternoon, silly considering I had a GCSE the next day, but I didn't care. We were at the park and I, had been staring at a broken bottle for almost an hour, she had been talking to me, but I didn't take in anything she was saying.
Then she put her head in my line of vision.

'What are you thinking about?' she asked,

'Whether it would hurt to run that piece of glass into my skin.'

She. looked at me shocked 'Are you crazy?' she snapped

'No just a slag' I said giggling.

'Fuck me, Sarah, you are like a nun compared to most girls around here' she said,

'I just hate being me, and that glass could end this all'
I said with tears filling in my eyes.

Mona put her arms around me and told me I was stupid, she said I was the bravest most beautiful person she had ever met.

That didn't make me feel any better, she then told me that I was stupid for even thinking about cutting my wrists.

'Who said anything about my wrists?' I asked her 'I was more thinking about distorting my face with it' I said smiling

'You are fucking crazy' she stated, 'You are pretty so why would you want to change that?' she asked with a concerned look on her face.

That's the problem I thought to myself. I didn't believe this would happen if I were a fat ugly girl.

Sweet Sixteen...

I had turned sixteen the day before my last exam, not that I did anything special. Birthdays were like any other day apart from getting a few bits from my mum in the morning and a few cards it was like any ordinary day. Mona thought it was crazy that I was sixteen and not even having a party, but even if I had wanted one it wasn't going to happen, we had just moved to a new house, only a few doors away. Mum was working every hour she could, and my dad was on even more crack cocaine than he was before, so we never had any money.

My birthday presents, were a pair of dark jeans, and Ellesse jacket and a training bra, at the age of sixteen I was still flat chested, and I was embarrassed as hell opening it up in front of my brothers. The twins were ten by this point, and any boobs or bras would make them giggle, so once I had opened my presents I took them straight upstairs. I had tried on my new clothes and everything fit me perfectly apart from my bra, that was always the way, no matter what style, they were still far too big for me.

Once I was dressed, and done my makeup, I decided I needed to do something, so I went out and didn't return home till six o'clock that evening.

When I did get back, mum was out at work, and my dad told me that, my dinner was in the microwave, so I sat in the kitchen and ate my dinner. When I finished, I decided to do the dishes and put them all away. Dad walked into the kitchen to see what the noise was

'What the fuck are you creeping for?' he asked

'I'm not; I just thought I would tidy up before I go back out' I replied,

'You're not going back out' he snapped back 'you can stay in and keep me company.'

That was the last thing I wanted, but I knew there was no point in trying to argue. Dads abuse of me was more beating nowadays than sexual, so I wasn't too worried as he seemed in a good enough mood, so after I had finished what I was doing, I went into the living room to get ready to watch the soaps.

Just as I sat down, dad had sent me upstairs to get the kids in bed so once they were settled, I decided to get undressed myself, no point in keeping my tight new jeans on if I wasn't allowed out anyway.

I had missed most of Emmerdale by the time I got back downstairs and just as I sat down on the sofa dad had asked me to make him a drink. So off I went into the kitchen to make his cup of tea, when I got back into the living room, dad had put porn on, I tried to act like I didn't notice, but he told me to sit beside him on the sofa.

I told him I needed to get my drink and he snapped at me telling me the sit down when he says so. I did what I was told. He then pulled me closer to him, put his arm around me and placed his hand on my bum. My nighty was in the way so he moved it and placed his hand under my knickers, so he could feel my flesh against his palm. Then using the other hand, he started rubbing himself. I honestly believed the abuse with him had stopped because this was the first time it had happened in months.

I was scared that now I was older that he would try and do more, but luckily enough after a few minutes he pushed me away, he said I didn't do it for him anymore. He was throwing the common insults at me like I was a slag, a whore and he kept saying I secretly loved what he did to me. He couldn't have been further away from the truth if he had tried. My skin has got used to crawling around him.

Leaving Home...

Nothing happened again after that night dad had the porn on, I was too old for him now, a pedophile likes the control they have over younger children and I think my dad could see he was losing the hold he had on me and since the rape. I had started to argue more, resulting in more beatings but I had got used to it, and in any situation, once you get too used to it, it becomes repetitive and boring. I was no longer scared of my dad, and I didn't care what he did to me anymore. To make sure he had less chance to start on me, I spent all day every day out, only returning home to get a bite to eat and going out again.

I had a full-time job working at a local factory making chocolate; it sounds a lot more glamorous than it was, I hated the job itself but loved the freedom it gave me and the wages at the end of the week. Not that I see most of my payments, with mum and especially dad still heavily addicted to crack most of my money was taken from me to feed their habit. So, I took a second job working in the evening at the hotel I had done my work experience at. I enjoyed my job but it was demanding work, the hours almost killed me after working all day in a sweaty factory. But I was trying my hardest to put money away for my big escape.

I had convinced myself I needed money to move, so I started saving in a tub underneath my bed. I must have saved over two hundred pounds when I returned home one day to find the tub rolling around the floor outside my front door, I ran over to pick it up but it was empty, all my money had gone.

I stormed into the house shouting about my find, and my dad told me it was my own fault that I should have put it in my back, he then started to question where I had the money from when I told him though I could tell he thought I was lying. I had asked if he knew where the money had gone and he looked down at his crack pipe.

'Doesn't go far' he said smirking at me.

I was ready to explode and stormed back out of the house. I made my way to the other end of the estate to where Katie was chilling with a few of our mates. She was seeing a boy called Dean.

He was an ugly looking thing with a balding head and eyes that looked far too big for his little head, but who was I to talk. I had been flirty with Simon all night. I had known Simon for over a year, but as he was almost ten years older than me I never looked twice at him, but I knew he fancied me, so I played along with it. I had told him previously about my crack head parents, so it was no surprise when I turned up angry that my dad had stolen my money.
Simon commented on me moving in with him and his cousin Vicky, I didn't get on with Victoria but the idea tempted me, we sat and had a smoke and about nine o'clock that evening Simon had walked me home.

Once we got the end of my street, we stopped, and I said my goodbyes.

'I was serious by the way' Simon said as I was walking away. I turned to face him, walking backward.

'What do you mean?'

He looked back at me and said, 'You are welcome to move into mine, we have plenty of room.'

I just laughed at him, 'Oh please don't tempt me.'

Dad was asleep when I got home, so I said goodnight to my mum who was lying down on the sofa with the TV on low and the lights off. She had slept on the couch most nights since Matthew was born, at the start, it was so the baby didn't disturb the rest of the house, but it had turned into a regular thing now, even though Matthew now slept upstairs she would stay downstairs.

The next morning, I got up for work, as usual, dad had asked what time I was due home, and if I had worked at the hotel that evening, I told him I was home for about six, and no I didn't work at the hotel on a Thursday night.
He then said I could stay for that evening.
I wasn't going to be staying in at all, by this point I was seventeen, and I knew I had more control over my life, so after work instead of going home, I had decided to go straight round Simon's. I knew he was in because he was a bum who didn't work, lived off benefits and smoked weed all day.

I knocked on the door, and he answered with a big grin on his face.

'Was you being serious when you said I could stay?' I asked,

'Of course, I was your daft mere, I would do anything to see that smile back on your face' was his reply.

So, with that, I smiled at him, batted my eyelids, and walked through to the living room.

Our mate Large was being weird, sat in the middle of the room with incense burning around him, he believed he was a vampire and convinced himself that he could do spells and stuff.

'He is trying to control the candle' Simon whispered in my ear.

So, we left him to it and went upstairs where the rest of the crew were skinning up and listening to music. To be honest, I hated all the heavy metal stuff they were listening to but the more I sat in the room, the more I got used to the screams of Cradle of Filth's frontman.
So that day it was decided that I was to move in and have the spare room, Simon knew I worked but said he didn't want my money. I was just to put a tenner in the electric once a week and buy my own food, so with everything sorted I just needed to find the right time to tell my parents I was moving out, which I wasn't looking forward to.

The moment to tell my parents came a few days later, it was the weekend, and I had returned home to get my dinner like planned, as soon as I walked in through the door, my dad had started bitching at me

'You use this fucking house like a hotel' he snapped
'Start spending more time at home, or you can move out' he continued.

I was already pissed off, so I told him 'I want to move out anyway.'

He sniggered 'And how do you expect to do that?'

I sat down at the table, all grown up, and explained where I was moving to. Dad just thought it was funny; he said I wouldn't last five minutes without my mum doing everything for me and that I wasn't allowed to come running back when it all went wrong, he said I was on my own and never to ask them for help again. This suited me, as I was just glad that I was finally able to get away from all this shit I had to cope with at home. I wasn't thinking about anyone but myself, not even my brothers, the way I saw it was this was the chance I had to get away, and I was taking it no matter what.

Mum tried that evening to talk me out of it, but I had made up my mind. I was finally moving out and was excited about the idea of overseeing my own life, and I was convinced that things would be a lot easier from this moment on.

In some respects, life was easier after that day, but my cursed twisted life was set to carry on...

To my readers <3

Thank you so much for taking the time to read this, I understand that some bits might have been hard to read, and trust me at times were hard to write. Initially, I started writing this book to help myself, it was a form of counseling for me, but once I had finished, I began to hope this story may be able to help someone else one day.

Unfortunately, abuse happens all the time, and sometimes it can be right underneath our noses, and we still won't see it. I hope if you, yourself or if you know someone going through a similar experience, my story will give you the courage to speak out... just as a book made me realize I needed to tell my own story xxx

I have recently published my second novel titled A Mile in my Own Shoes © This book continues my story from the age of 17 to 30... 'Fingers crossed this book has left you interested enough to want to know more about my life, and let's just say it doesn't get any easier the older I get....

Where will my journey end © the final story in this sequel will be available in the winter of 2017-2018

Thank you for helping me share my story xxx

'Everything Happens for a reason.'

or so they say...

My Life in His Hands

By Sarah Louise Rosmond xoxo

Made in the USA
Lexington, KY
30 December 2017